click!

Choosing Love...One Frame at a Time

click!

Choosing Love...One Frame at a Time

INCLUDING SHORT STORIES BY
Tom Robbins, Kathleen McGowan,
Ram Dass, Dr. Joe Dispenza,
Kenny Loggins and others.

Published by
Agape Media International, LLC
Los Angeles, California
www.AgapeMe.com

Hay House, Inc.
P.O. Box 5100
Carlsbad, CA 92018-5100
www.hayhouse.com

Cover Jacket Design: Amy Thornton
Text Design: Rebecca Finkel
Production Layout: Launa Fujimoto
Editors: Donna DeNomme, Jordan Paul and Barbara Munson
Executive in Charge of Publication: Stephen Powers
Jacket Artwork: Aperture @ Istockphoto.com; Rays of Light @ photos.com
Photograph of Author on Front Cover: Cynthia James
Photograph of Author on Back Flap: Stanley Strauss
Back Cover Photographs: Carl Studna
Interior Photographs: Carl Studna except for Little Carl,
Photographer Unknown

ISBN: 978-1-4019-4089-8

Printed on recycled paper.

*This book is dedicated
to all the teachers and educators of the world
who provide tireless service to inspire and ignite
the imagination and innate wisdom
of the young and old.*

contents

Photographs ix

Foreword by Michael Bernard Beckwith xi

Acknowledgments xv

Preface xvii

Introduction 1

Practicing "Just Being" 7

   A Soul Lost/A Truth Told, by Kenny Loggins 13

What Does It Mean to "Be Seen"? 17

   From Beige to Beautiful, by Carol Ratcliffe Alm 25

To Trust or Not to Trust? 27

   Capturing Joy, by Kathleen McGowan 39

Creating a Safe Space 43

What Is the Essential Moment? 51

   In the Silence, by Cynthia James 63

Now You See It, Now You Don't 67

   Interview with Ram Dass 71

Is Being Self-Conscious a Bad Thing? 79

   See and Be Seen, by Leilani Raashida Henry 85

Releasing Judgment and Opening to the Broader Picture 89

   I Look Good, by Karen Drucker 97

Living in the Tao 103

   The Present, by Dr. Joe Dispenza 109

Remembering Self-Love 117

   Photos of My Life, by Dan Kessler 125

What Are You Hiding?. 131

    The Feather, by Raymond Aaron. 135

Reclaiming Self-Expression and Freedom 139

    Canon Fodder, by Tom Robbins 147

Wild Goose Chase 151

    Ageless Beauty, by Marian Head. 159

Every Picture Tells a Story. 161

    Embracing the Pieces, One Picture at a Time,

    by Zemirah Jazwierska 171

Creating a New Life Story. 175

    Snapshot Memories, by Donna DeNomme 181

The Outer Reflecting the Inner. 185

    Guiding Light, by Sharon Hampton 191

You Are the Light 193

Contributors 199

Endorsement Contributors 203

About the Author 205

photographs

PAGE XIII   *At One.* Michael Bernard Beckwith, Pine, Colorado, 2008

PAGE 5   *Bhutanese Girl.* A festival in Thimphu, Bhutan, 1999

PAGE 8   *Just Being.* Carl Studna/Self-Portrait, At home in my bathroom mirror, Los Angeles, California, 1972

PAGE 19   *Paris Birdman.* In front of Sacré-Cœur Basilica, Paris, France, 1994

PAGE 30   *Evolution of Loving.* Walter and Carla Chotzen, Oahu, Hawaii, 1995

PAGE 34   *The Red Piano.* Elton John, Las Vegas, Nevada, 2008

PAGE 48   *Little Carl.* Photographer unknown, Los Angeles, California, 1958

PAGE 54   *Wildest Dream.* Paul McCartney, Nicasio, California, 1992

PAGE 57   *Synthesis Dialogues.* The Dalai Lama, Dharamsala, India, 1999

PAGE 75–78   *Inner Life Reflections.* Ram Dass, San Anselmo, California, 1989

PAGE 82   *A Mentor.* George Harrison, Hollywood, California, 1991

PAGE 91   *Rebirth.* Pingree Park, Colorado, 2010

PAGE 114   *Living in the Present.* Dr. Joe Dispenza, Pine, Colorado, 2009

PAGE 119   *Holy Chihuahua.* Santa Barbara, California, 2010

PAGE 132   *Shining Light.* Marianne Williamson, Lakewood, Colorado, 2005

PAGE 137   *College days:* Carl Studna/Self-Portrait, Cotati, California, 1977

PAGE 143   *Youthful Abandon.* Dunleary, Ireland, 2010

PAGE 149   *Typical Day at Home.* Tom Robbins, La Conner, Washington, 1983

PAGE 157   *In Home Garden.* Laura Huxley, Hollywood, California, 1994

PAGE 170   *Country Glee.* Sebastopol, California, 1978

PAGE 180   *Embracing the Dusk.* Santa Rosa, California, 1977

PAGE 189   *Messenger of Light.* Deepak Chopra, Westminster, Colorado, 2008

PAGE 197   *Illumination.* St. Peter's Basilica, the Vatican, 1979

foreword

By Michael Bernard Beckwith

Artistic perceptivity is limitless. And when it's related to photography, angling the camera and pressing the button are secondary to the inner, perceptive eye of the photographer.

I have known Carl Studna, both personally and as a member of my spiritual community, the Agape International Spiritual Center, for twenty-three years. Throughout those years, he has photographed me countless times. When a selection of my photographs is submitted for public relations purposes, Carl's are most often "first pick."

I've always known the reason why this occurs is beyond the tilt of my head, the smile on my face, my wardrobe choices or the photo's backdrop. It is Carl's inner perception that creates the space for him to clearly see and capture the essential essence of his subjects. What intuitively resonates at his core being about what he perceives infuses the photographs he takes.

Carl's work is best described by the wise observation of another artist, Mies van der Rohe, a pioneer of modern architecture, who said, "God is in the details." It is the wealth of Carl's inner life—his spiritual practices—that inform his work. His capacity to be present to the freshness, to the awe of the moment, to intuitively connect to his photo's subject, are born of genuinely loving, honoring and respecting what he sees through the lens of the camera.

Click is the result of the wisdom Carl has gathered through his use of the camera as a tool of clear seeing with the eye of the heart. With every click, he catches the rich textures of humanity's yearnings, aspirations, sorrows, joys, secrets, revelations and triumphs. Carl's own stories, along with those from a diverse collection of guest authors, will open the eyes, minds and hearts of readers to discover how the power within each immediate moment invites them into a way of perceiving the preciousness of being a spiritual being having a human incarnation.

—MICHAEL BERNARD BECKWITH
Los Angeles, California

acknowledgments

It all began when my dear friend, Bob Brenner, told me, "Carl…you need to write a book!" Thank you, Bob, for planting the seed at the perfect moment. My dear Elana Golden, thank you for being the nurturing writing teacher who sparked within me a greater love for the craft of writing. I'm deeply grateful to Donna DeNomme, Jordan Paul and Barbara Munson for dedicating their time and talent to the editing of this project. Donna and Jordan, your unconditional support and friendship have been instrumental. Amy Thornton and Rebecca Finkel, your artistry with the book design fully matches my inner vision…you are the best! Launa Fujimoto, I thank you from the bottom of my heart for your steadfast dedication at getting all of the final design and layout touches in their perfect order. Arielle Ford, you continue to serve as an angelic conduit of support in my life. Your long-term friendship is deeply valued. Stephen Powers, from the moment I began discussing the concept of *Click* with you, I could see that you truly caught the vision. I couldn't imagine a more respectful and supportive publisher. Thanks to all those at Hay House involved with the printing, marketing and distribution of this project. Your resources and experience are invaluable. Deep appreciation goes out to Bill Gladstone for believing in this book and serving as my perfect literary agent. I extend sincere gratitude to Cathy and Gary Hawk for your radiant coaching and keeping me on track. Betsy Wiersma, your expertise in helping to refine my presentation as an engaging speaker on this material has been most effective and appreciated. I'm sincerely grateful to Jack Canfield and the Transformational Leadership Council. Your commitment to being the best you can be and giving the fullness of your talent continues to serve as an inspiring force in my life. My dear friends, James and Debra Rouse, you have been amazing in your constant commitment to my well-being and the success of this project. A mighty thank you goes out to my long-term friend, Michael Torphy, for your constant support and presence as my monthly visioning partner. I'm so touched by all of the writers who have contributed stories to this project. Your willingness to unconditionally give of yourselves has made a lasting impression in my heart and on these very pages. Michael Beckwith, your wisdom and inspired spiritual guidance have served as a cornerstone throughout the years in tremendously influencing my deeper awakening to the Universal One. Hugs, laughter and smiles extend out to all of my dear friends who have always seen the highest in me. My love and thanksgiving go out to my parents, Harlan and Reona, for raising me to be a loving and compassionate man, and to my sister, Diane, for a lifelong bond of support. Lastly, I wish to thank my wife, Cynthia James, for serving as a role model in so many areas of my life. You inspire me and raise me up!

preface

From the moment the seed was planted to write a book, the information began to flood onto the page without an ounce of effort. It's as if a lifetime of observation wished to have a voice and I simply said, "YES."

I've been in love with the craft of photography since age fifteen. Throughout my entire adulthood, it has served as a vehicle for expression, particularly for reflecting the awesome beauty and light of this world and its inhabitants. I've witnessed areas of success, having the honor of meeting and photographing many luminaries who inspired and contributed to shaping my life choices. I've stood in front of hundreds of people with my camera and learned to be honoring with each soul who offers their trust in me.

Over time, it's become very clear how vulnerable a position it is for each person to muster up the willingness to be seen through this unique medium. Without consciously realizing it, I gradually began to raise my degree of skill, not just in the craft of photography, but in having greater compassion for my subjects. My level of intuition was being sharpened and I was *feeling* into the perfect moment to click the picture. That moment of the let go… when the ego was taking a break!

I'm not sure when the shift happened, but at some point my role grew from simply taking people's pictures into fully honoring each individual, and

I was naturally showing up and cultivating a relaxed, safe and enjoyable atmosphere. I began to see each person's essence emanating through their eyes and through their unique way of being. I could never get bored because each individual brought a presence and energy to the session that was unlike anyone else. Somewhere along the path, I experienced a metamorphosis and was no longer just a photographer…I became a revealer of light.

I began to realize that if people could feel comfortable, trusting and fully present in being themselves in front of a camera, embodying these qualities in their day-to-day life should be a piece of cake! I'm absolutely clear that the key element that must be present to reflect an authentic image in every moment of the camera's click is love. When we are steeped in the pure essence of loving ourselves, everything in our lives must align with this atmosphere of wholeness.

I am most grateful that you are about to join me in exploring what it means to live a life steeped in choices that honor your fullest of expression. Using the example of being in front of a camera as an ultimate metaphor for how authentically you show up in your life, may you glean the gems that will serve you brilliantly in providing a broader stroke of freedom throughout your life choices and in your ability to fully love and be loved.

in love

Carl Studna

introduction

CLICK

What thoughts, feelings and desires are present in that essential moment when the camera's aperture opens and closes? Are you present in that moment or wanting to be somewhere else? Be someone else? Look like someone else?

> **CLICK** ...love or separation?
>
> **CLICK** ...honor or judgment?
>
> **CLICK** ...breathe or constrict?
>
> **CLICK** ...be present or mask?
>
> **CLICK** ...express or withdraw?
>
> **CLICK** ...shine or shrink?

What does it mean to fully bask in the moment of the **CLICK?**

I love having my picture taken! How often do you hear people proclaim this statement with glee and conviction? I imagine that most of you love having your picture taken as much as going to the dentist or the proctologist! That's the consensus I've heard during my thirty-plus years of photographing people.

My first vivid memory of having my picture taken was a family portrait when I was four years old. After setting up his lights and camera in our living room, the photographer stuck us in a rigid pose. The last thing I wanted was being told to be still. I wanted to bolt off the couch and run around outside. I wanted to be free, not pinned down and ordered to be quiet and constrained. I'm sure that I was a royal pain in the butt as I squirmed and complained! I surely did not see any value in this experience, nor any purpose whatsoever that made it interesting or worthwhile.

Shortly after this fiasco, I began watching the television show, *Love That Bob*. Bob Cummings played a hip, bachelor photographer who appeared carefree and quite the ladies' man. The show always began with an upbeat theme song and as the song ended Bob entered. As he lifted his camera and took a picture of the viewing audience he would say, "Smile, I think you're going to like this picture!" This carefree, happy, creative adult set an early childhood imprint that taking people's pictures could be fun. He sure looked a lot happier than my father or any other male adults in my life.

This TV show and the positive reference to having a camera in your face was likely the only time as a child that I witnessed having one's picture taken as an enjoyable act. The rest of the time it felt like an obligation or something that needed to be done in a certain way.

In the fifties and early sixties, the photographer's protocol was to give the command, "Say Cheese," and everyone in front of the camera would respond in unison with their artificial, plastered-on smiles. This technique must have been invented by some brainchild as a simple way of getting people to flex their mouths in the form of a smile while saying this silly word. Clearly, it was not about invoking natural smiles that would look authentic on film. Imagine if there had been a different scenario to effectively get people to authentically laugh and smile. If that approach had caught on, perhaps we might actually enjoy having our pictures taken and see it as an opportune moment to playfully interact and let our light shine.

It's fascinating to think about some of the words that are used when describing a photographic moment. Phrases like "having your picture taken" evoke the sense of something being taken from you. In certain indigenous cultures, it is believed that when someone takes your picture, they are capturing your Soul. Think about how often we use the word "capture" to describe documenting a specific moment with the camera. "I captured you in the most hilarious pose you could imagine." For years, I've made a conscious effort to avoid using the word "capture" by replacing it with words like document or reveal. I'm still searching for other words that do justice to this act. If you have any suggestions, I'd love to hear them!

What if every time someone was photographing you, you experienced it as a moment of self-honoring, even if that was not the intention of the person behind the camera? Feel like a stretch? Each time I travel to a developing country that has not been indoctrinated by western values, I'm moved by how simply and seamlessly the people respond to my request to take their portraits. When my wife and I traveled to remote areas of Bhutan several years ago, almost everyone that I approached to request a photo had a similar response. They would look at me, perhaps a bit perplexed, not understanding why I would care to have a picture of them, but nod yes and feel completely comfortable with the process. I didn't ask them to smile or do anything other than be present. They would simply look into the camera and show up without any seeming concerns, thoughts or agendas. I was acutely aware that they were not conditioned to feel like they needed to be a certain way in front of a camera. They showed no signs whatsoever of being concerned about their looks, how they were dressed or whether they were doing it "right." They only smiled when they genuinely felt like smiling.

Consequently, the portraits of these Bhutanese people convey such an authentic presence. As you look into their eyes, there is an openness that invites you to travel deeply into their hearts and souls. This is the same kind and giving way that we felt when talking with them *(those that spoke English)*. We learned that in their culture they are governed by a king and by a spiritual advisor. Most of the country's people practice Tibetan Buddhism and you can actually feel a calm, still presence in the air. Many of the country's decisions are made jointly between the king and his spiritual advisor. What a concept! It's no wonder that these people feel so comfortable in front of a camera, for they have nothing to hide. Presumably, they don't associate their self-worth with what they look like, what they own or what kind of job they have. There seems to be a deeper spiritual value that's not based on outer circumstances or appearances that govern their lives.

Once you recognize that all of life is an "inside job," looking outside for answers is fruitless. When I bring myself to a still place of high-level listening, the inner wisdom always guides me in the direction that I need to go. So, how does this tie into having *your* picture taken?

My objective in writing this book is using this unique medium, photography, to serve as an opportunity to reflect. Every time that we are in front of the lens we can assess what's truly important and muster up the willingness to be real. May this photographic reflection serve as a reminder of who we really are at the core of our nature. May these writings hit upon a deep, resonant chord in each life path and inspire the perfect places within to recalibrate, bringing a fuller sense of wholeness, freedom and self-expression.

Being in front of a camera is a method for receiving instant feedback on where our thoughts are being placed. How are we feeling about ourselves? What "false" values are we placing on ourselves that take us away from being fully present, radiant and alive while in front of the camera? What does it look like to be fully authentic in expressing our true selves, in this very moment, while being in front of a device that objectively documents whatever moment of expression is present?

practicing "just being"

I grew up witnessing my father constantly trying to be successful in order to feel good about himself and meet my mother's high needs and desires. Of course these desires were never fully met because she kept looking for a sense of security from outer circumstances and material goods. Nevertheless, I was raised with a strong model that taught me how necessary it was to "put my nose to the grindstone" in an effort to make things happen.

Entering my teenage years, I began questioning my parents and their generation's values, and vowed *(as most teenagers do)* that I would never be like them. I took the route of living a more alternative lifestyle, embracing the "hippie" movement that was flourishing in California during the early seventies. I was initiated into Transcendental Meditation at age seventeen, completed the EST Training at age twenty, and was schooled at Sonoma State University, where most of the teachers practiced an experiential approach to learning. My world became devoted to deepening my awareness of my choices in each moment. I vowed to make decisions that would provide a great sense of freedom in my life, including not being tied down to a day-to-day job or any obligation that would have me feeling the least bit enslaved.

I married Leslie, a kindred spirit straight out of college, and moved back to Los Angeles to launch a photography business. There, once again I vowed to never allow my business or life choices to drag me down and compromise my freedom and my integrity. Yet the truth is that during the five years of my marriage to Leslie, I was so absorbed in trying to build a business while so desperately trying to be successful that I lost touch with some of my most important core values. I allowed the old conditioning of fear to cloud my priorities and to gradually cause a breakdown in communication and intimacy.

Even with all of my previous training to teach me otherwise, I jumped into the fast-moving pace of Los Angeles with its own set of success values and began to lose sight of what it meant to slow down and listen from the inside out. It took the drama of Leslie leaving our marriage for me to wake up *(after months and months of deep pain and introspection)* and reassess my beliefs and life choices. Once more, I vowed to never allow fear to cloud and guide my choices ever again *(or at least not for long!)*. From that point forward, beginning in my late twenties, I've managed to keep a pretty good perspective on the necessity to tell the truth, at all costs. I've found that if I do not speak the truth to others and myself, it will eventually come out in a far more painful and dramatic fashion.

When we are truly living in the present moment, all that can show up is a sense of spaciousness, free of judgment or any form of separation. I recently had a friend ask me, "Can I really let go of control while having my picture taken?" Absolutely, but it takes being mindful and trusting that there is truly nothing you need to do other than simply show up and BE you!

So how does this tie in to Just Being? I love the simple yet profound message at the core of Eckhart Tolle's teachings: fear cannot reside in gratitude.

Cultivating this state of practicing the presence requires a deepening in faith, a willingness to be vigilantly mindful of catching any beliefs that are based in old fears, like my father's certainty that success can "only come through great effort and hardship." Once aware of the "false" belief, we can begin the process of releasing it with love, knowing that it simply has no purpose any longer and replacing it with affirmative statements that are aligned with our true values and beliefs.

I find that the greatest constant thought that keeps me from being still and listening from that clear and receptive frequency is the notion that I need to be "doing" something in this moment other than simply being. At the core of this belief is the conclusion that doing presides over being. It is in this moment of thought that I must challenge the belief and remind myself that it is not true.

While writing portions of this book I was on a cruise ship, sitting in my cabin looking out at the vast Pacific Ocean. All that was present were the moving and glistening ripples in the sea, the horizon line, a pale blue sky and white billowy clouds; all moving from left to right across the large windows framing this moving picture. Sounds pretty idyllic for an environment to "just be" without all the distractions of everyday life coming at me from every direction. I'd say it's about as idyllic as one could ask for, yet I sat there with moments of thinking, "What's best to write about next? How shall

I tie this in? What format do I wish to use? Blah, blah blah... All of these thoughts were slowing down the process, rather than simply allowing the creative spark to have its way through me from moment to moment. What might it look and feel like to be in the creative flow, that state of allowance where information and expression simply become One?

I release it to the nothingness from where it came and allow my attention to go back to the stillness where peace, wholeness and grace reside, being perfectly guided by the Infinite Intelligence that lives, breathes and sustains each of us. The more frequently that I catch this belief and lovingly choose to release it, I find that it has nowhere to latch on, no resting place.

Sometimes I experience this fluid state of being when practicing my morning meditations. I'll be placing my attention on my breath, continually letting go of passing thoughts. In these moments that Deepak Chopra, in his book *The Seven Spiritual Laws of Success,* calls, "The Gap," I am in a state of not thinking, simply being. I find that as I continue to allow more of these "being" moments to have their way during my meditations and throughout the day, it is from them that the clearest insights and direction enter my consciousness. It's a Catch 22 of sorts because I can't try to make this happen. It must reveal itself from a state of allowance, which lives in an entirely different paradigm than how most of us were raised.

Now, imagine practicing Just Being in front of a camera. What a great tool and moment of opportunity to be present with any old thoughts that surface telling you that you're not enough. Concerns that you're too fat, too thin, that your nose is too big, too small, that you have too many wrinkles, or that your smile is not flattering. The list goes on and on. How would it be to completely love yourself for exactly who you are in that moment, in a perfect place of self-honoring with nothing to do, simply be? As a photographer, I know how to access this authentic place and profile it through my camera lens. Walk with me as I show you the way to "Click," be present with where you are in the moment. It's time to release the need to control or manipulate your circumstances in order to have your life look a certain way, and instead open to the creative fullness of the moment and honor your ever-present, inner guidance.

A Soul Lost / A Truth Told

By Kenny Loggins

Believe it or not, some cultures still believe that to allow your picture to be taken is to allow your soul to be "captured," as if the soul has been stolen forever. So they run from the photographer as if from the devil himself, for how can a soul find eternal life if it is trapped within a stranger's small black box? How indeed?

And I wonder…how has such a myth persisted for almost two hundred years? Is it possible that some aspect of truth is peeking out from behind the superstitions of the primitive mind?

Throughout history we have certainly seen many examples of a photographer capturing a glimpse of a subject's soul, perhaps a "piece of one's soul," if you will, for the rest of us to see. It's as if the "soul" of the subject was frozen in time, a moment captured eternally within that box, printed onto the paper, someone's emotions caught in a kind of perpetual "still life"…*still alive*, shown to us exactly as the subject of the photograph "was" at that precise moment in time, *forever*. Glimpsing what they were feeling, thinking…their optimism or their despair, their faith or their unquenchable desires. The young actress caught in the act of being, say, twenty-one years old and gorgeous, narcissistic, affluent and ambitious. Or perhaps forty-five and fearful, tired, still trying desperately to be self-absorbed, but losing the belief that that's all there is anymore. Caught by the camera in the unconscious act of seeing her immortality slip silently away, day by day, losing one's religion, one's reason for being, in one click of the shutter.

I've often wondered, why is a day spent as the subject of a photo session so damned exhausting? It's simple enough work. I just sit and stare at the lens as if it's my oldest friend, smiling with all my heart, doing my best to feel a kind of kinship to the hidden viewer miles from the lens, or indeed, to the photographer him/herself. Theoretically, it shouldn't be any more difficult than spending a day at the beach with a dear friend. Certainly Carl and I have been close friends for many years now, and still…

But it isn't that, really, a day at the beach. It's damned hard work, and by the end of a day before the lens, I'm in need of at least a few hours of rest. But why?

Some might say that it's the exhaustion of trying so hard to constantly put one's best foot forward, pouring all your essence into an inanimate object for five or six hours. Somewhat akin to hanging out at a party with nothing but strangers for an entire evening, making small talk, being unrelentingly charming. That much energy expended pretending to be someone like-able is just plain fatiguing. Perhaps that's all there is to it?

Or perhaps it's exhausting trying to keep aspects of ourselves *hidden* from the all-seeing lens? Don't we all fear there's something to hide, really? Some part of us we'd rather not get caught on film? In a way, perhaps a definition of "greatness" is the willingness, the absolute courage to show it all, right there on film, for the world to see and empathize with. To judge. To relate to. To understand. To revile?

Then again, could that just as easily be the definition of "foolishness," of an unbridled, "bulletproof" ego, brazenly daring us to see through the facade? The very definition of a politician. Who's to say?

But aren't the most compelling photographs the most honest ones? Take Diane Arbus's images of the lost and outcast. Those with nothing to hide. Those with nothing to lose. Their eyes tell of their lives spent hunted and running, alone and forsaken, and of their courage to keep on when many others would have simply given it up.

I suspect even Annie Leibovitz's star-studded, famous photos show more than what I imagine many of her subjects, those denizens of Hollywood, might consciously have wanted us to see. Surely a piece of the soul was stolen for *that* shot?

So my job, as the subject of Carl's or anyone's photograph, is simply to **be**, to be myself at that particular moment in time, to relinquish a bit of my soul for the viewer to merge with, to be willing to let my image tell the same story as my music. After all, a life spent dancing with art must, by nature, be a life of revelations, a life of no secrets, a life spent believing that we are really all the same, all of the same mud and blood, all struggling with the same journey towards each other. To tell the truth artistically is to tell OUR story. So why not smile and say "cheese"? I have nothing to hide, really. Here is my reality. Here is my music. Here is my life before you, just as you might wish to pretend isn't actually happening to you, too. Here, my friend, is my soul. Can you relate?

And somehow, remarkably, the very moment I offer it up to the altar of the camera, so it is magically reborn, exhilarated, anew, free from the fear of being seen.

Still, I do hate getting my picture taken. It's so damned exhausting. I suspect the day I am truly at peace with the camera, I will be well on the road to self-realization, at ease with however I am seen, with or without a camera. And perhaps, in this way, future photo sessions will become my signposts on my road to freedom?

what does it mean to "be seen"?

Many years ago I was en route to Tijuana, Mexico, to photograph an up-and-coming band performing at a wild, over-the-border nightclub. I parked my car on the US side of the border thinking it would be safer there. What I didn't consider was my own safety!

On my way back from the club at 2:00 a.m., the streets were sparse with people and cars as I began to cross a freeway overpass. I spotted two teenage Mexican men being rowdy with each other at the top of the overpass, so I crossed the street to walk past them with some distance. Out of my peripheral vision, I could see them beginning to cross the street and they were clearly following me. I was their target. I began to speed up my pace and they picked up theirs as well; in fact they were gaining on me. In that moment, I had an illuminating thought: "If I continue to act in fear and play the role of a victim, they will gladly pursue me and be victorious." So, as they came up from behind me, I chose to turn around and greet them.

Without thinking, I tapped into a nonlinear, compassionate place within and inquired, "Just tell me what you need." In that moment, I was very aware that the game had changed. I was no longer a victim being stalked, I was a person genuinely caring about these two young men, and I truly did wish to give them what they needed if able.

One of the guys, likely the leader of the two, looked at me in a stunned and slightly confused way, paused and said, "Do you have any 'shrooms? We just want some 'shrooms!" This was slang for psychedelic mushrooms. Clearly he thought that I'd be a good candidate for scoring some free drugs as my hair was quite long and I was wearing a backpack *(which happened to store my camera inside)*. I replied with all honesty that I didn't have any 'shrooms, but if I had, I would have gladly offered them over. He paused for a moment, and I believe that he could sense my sincerity. In a very demanding tone he yelled out, "Walk on, Holmes, walk on!" With that, I walked on ahead of them for another few minutes to my car as they continued to follow behind me.

Once I got inside my car, the fear began to creep in, all of the "what ifs"! But the truth is, the "what ifs" had no weight in this situation because I chose to be real with them. I'm crystal clear that I was at a choice point when they came up behind me and I could have either acted out of fear or out of love. I chose to cut through the fear and simply show up genuinely caring about their needs. In that moment, I fully saw them as human beings that were in some sort of pain and I really wanted to be there for them and honor their needs. Looking back on this situation, I'm certain that my safety and my belongings remained intact because I chose to care and express love while in the midst of a seeming life-threatening drama.

So how do we cultivate this awareness on a more consistent basis? Well, I'm a true believer in the Law of Attraction that tells us whatever thoughts we cultivate deeply enough in consciousness will out-picture in the material world. As we fully see others as whole and recognize their unique gifts,

the world around us can only respond in kind and you'll start noticing that everyone around you is seeing, acknowledging and supporting your talents. Make this a priority in your daily life and you will begin to feel recognized and appreciated for who you really are and for all that you offer in the world.

There are so many opportunities throughout each day to take a moment and truly see the value of the person in front of you, whether it's the person who bags your groceries, a bank teller, a gardener, your best friend or your spouse. If you really wish to stretch and be adventurous, practice seeing the wholeness with someone who rubs you the wrong way. Once this perspective and practice become a way of seeing the world, you are on the road to mastery as it becomes more and more evident that, in reality, there is nobody against us, just varying perspectives on how each of us view the world.

I've come to the conclusion that anyone who I perceive as being cruel, manipulative or unconscious with me is somebody who's in pain. To harm another, whether through bodily injury, words, lies or betrayal, requires acting out of pain. Think about it, how could anyone do harm to another if they were feeling fully loved, honored and provided for? It wouldn't happen because they would be so in touch with their own core of compassion for others and the world. There would be no sense of separation with others and they would only want the best for everyone. If you are someone who deeply loves your parents or your children, you only want the best for them, right? You would not wish to see any harm done to those you love.

What if it's a grand illusion that there is any separation in the world? What if we cared as deeply for those impoverished "out there" in a third-world country *(or in this country, for that matter)* as we do for our own families? I'm not suggesting that individually we can provide for everyone in the world who's in need. We can, however, see everyone as a part of the whole and bring compassion to every thought and action in our daily lives. We can know that our loving thoughts do make a difference and choose various projects and charities to offer our time or financial support. We can simply bring love to all regions and people throughout the world who are in pain.

Imagine that you're walking in the woods and you come across a little girl who has lost her way. She's curled up against a tree, shaking and whimpering. She can barely speak as she's so tired from hours of crying. You kneel down next to her and assure her that everything will be alright; that she is now safe with all needs provided. She looks up at you with such sweet, loving eyes and you are reminded that there is nothing more important in the world than this moment of giving loving care.

Now imagine being in an argument with someone who you consider a close friend. She has betrayed your trust by gossiping with another person in a way that feels cruel and disrespectful. Your first instinct might be to feel deeply hurt and then, almost instantly, that hurt turns into anger. Out of your anger, you might let everybody know what a complete fraud this ex-friend is. Fueled by your pain, you might make it your current mission in life to discredit this person because you want her to hurt as much as you do. This is an askew way of looking for justice because nobody wins and everyone feels hurt. This is why we have wars in the world!

Now picture another scenario. In the midst of this argument, you begin to see your friend as that lost little girl in the woods, feeling so alone and scared. You're not thinking of yourself because you know that you are fully loved and valued. There is nothing that threatens you or causes any form of reaction. You begin to see your friend as lost and in pain. Clearly, why else would anyone act in such a dishonoring way if she was not in such pain herself? Just as you felt nothing but compassion for that young child in the woods, you deeply feel your friend's pain and speak your truth from that perspective.

What questions do you ask and what do you want her to know? What does an authentic conversation look like that is simply focused on revealing the truth that's present? You might serve as a beacon of light for this person and reflect back where she is holding onto fear and pain. You might remind your friend of the wholeness at her core, truly seeing who she is underneath her reactive personality. If she's open, you might engage in a dialogue that explores the level of fear *(masked as insecurity)* that must be present for her to act with such disregard for your feelings. Perhaps you discuss how the building of trust and integrity in relationship serves as the cornerstone for growth in developing close relationships. With a clear loving heart, you might determine that this can no longer be a close friendship because the foundation of trust has been broken and you see that you're both walking very different paths. Sometimes, self-honoring choices are not easy.

I call the camera a revealer of truth. Whether it's a person, a landscape or a still life, the camera documents the truth of where it's being pointed. So, isn't it time that you allow the camera to be your friend? What if the camera's deepest desire is for you to be fully seen as the magnificent, radiant, talented and perfect person that you really are?

If you really believed this, how would you be in front of the camera? Perhaps you'd regard it as a fantastic opportunity to be seen for who you really are. Being seen, whether by an intimate partner, our boss at work or the checkout woman at the supermarket, feeds the same need and desire. We all wish to be authentically recognized for our uniqueness and for being perfect, just the way that we are. Imagine how fearless you would be if in every moment and throughout every situation in your life, you knew without a shadow of a doubt that every person you met fully saw your unique gifts and your wholeness. The floodgates would be wide open and you'd be unstoppable. There would be no limiting thoughts in your awareness because you'd know that everyone truly sees and supports your grandest expression!

What if you saw the camera lens as your beloved reflecting back to you the fullness of love, praise and devotion? This might sound like a stretch, but what better way than through the practice of being in front of a camera to empower the reminder that you are always whole and perfect? It sure beats resisting the process every time that a camera is pointed in your direction! Now is the opportune time to be seen—really seen—in front of the camera.

From Beige to Beautiful

The power of a photograph

By Carol Ratcliffe Alm

For the first fifty years of my life, I thought of myself as beige. Blending in and not standing out was the norm even through my successful corporate life. A longstanding message from childhood was a continual reminder that I shouldn't be too much, or say too much or do too much, and it was cemented with the understanding that I was clearly not beautiful. My beige-ness did not stop me from advancing through the ranks to senior vice president and executive director roles, but I considered myself as not photogenic and shied away from any PR photographs, family photos, vacation photos because I was certain that these images would only confirm the truth of my un-beauty and my non-beauty.

At some point on my journey, I began to realize that I could acknowledge that I was beautiful on the inside. If I radiated who I was rather than what I looked like, I could be beautiful. At 5' 9" with now silver white hair, I knew that when I entered a room or a meeting both men and women looked. But I felt like an oddity and not a beauty. Another small step forward came with the sense that I could imagine myself as elegant, still not beautiful, but no longer beige. I started to experiment with color beyond black, navy and camel corporate colors—still no photographs though, for fear of capturing and affirming my not beauty. In my entire corporate life, I'd only submitted to one photography session, fearful that people would focus on what I looked like and that what I looked like in a picture was a projection of my not-enough self.

Then, several years ago, the opportunity came forth to have a session with a world-class photographer, known for his talent in capturing the *essence of a person*. Maybe I could take another small step into visual imagery and really move through another layer of photographic fear. What was most important was to be able to trust the man with the camera. To put my "self," my image of not beautiful, in the hands of this professional who had photographed so very many beautiful people was close to terrifying. He would without a doubt see my un-beauty and feel sorry for me, but do the best that he could.

With humor, warmth, compassion and unbelievable skill, this man created a space for me to be me on film. He pulled forth and captured a stunning woman with beautiful eyes and an engaging smile. And most importantly, he created the photographs that finally allowed me to see, and to believe, what others had seen all along, that I am beautiful. This dramatic shift in my personal persona created a new listening as well; when others told me that I was beautiful, I now knew that they were speaking the truth. I actually believed them—and still do.

I'm no longer beige, but turquoise and sea foam green and rose and pink and blue and peach and coral. When I stand in front of groups to speak, I know what they see. They see the reflection of an authentic, powerful, compassionate woman whose work in the world is complemented by her beauty, her elegance and her grace. The gift of my beauty was defined and confirmed in the photographs by a man who saw who I am and helped me to believe it. I am eternally grateful for those pictures and for remembering who I really am.

to trust or not to trust?

Someone recently asked me, "Is it presumptuous to consider the camera lens to be my lover?" I say, whatever works! The lens can be your lover, a mirror of your perfection, the grace of God or your favorite chocolate cake! Whatever you wish to place as a positive association with this mechanical instrument. The camera is impartial; it simply reflects where we are placing our attention.

Years ago, as I was developing a friendship with noted singer/songwriter Kenny Loggins, he shared with me an experience that to this day continues to have a profound impact on my life. Kenny was in the depths of a new, blossoming love with his wife, Julia. The album, *Leap of Faith*, had recently been released, which was a brilliant compilation of songs about their love and his love of family. As Kenny and I sat one late afternoon in his hot tub, I stared out at the horizon of the Pacific Ocean and he began sharing a most intimate and profound experience.

He spoke of times when he and Julia were in the act of lovemaking and their connection was so strong as they gazed into each other's eyes. They witnessed a profound level of presence and raw vulnerability through this intimate act. While exploring the depths of the soul through each other's eyes, they experienced their partner's joy, pain and sense of oneness. They witnessed the multilayered dimensions and expressions of their beloved unfolding before them.

Kenny continued to share with me that during one of their acts of love, he stared into Julia's eyes and thought, "I'd love to be able to document the sheer power, presence and radiance that I see streaming through Julia's eyes right now." He turned to me and asked what I thought about a photography book that would document this intimate, vulnerable and powerful reflection of love as seen through a diverse series of couples devoted to growth and conscious partnership. In that moment, I realized that he was really testing the waters to see if I might be the right person to take on this courageous project. Over the course of the next week, it became clear that if I approached this project from a deep place of reverence, I could bring a level of trust into the sacred environment of each couple that would serve as a reminder of the preciousness and sanctity of their connection with each other. And that is exactly what transpired.

Over the course of several years, I was deeply honored to be with a series of loving, devoted couples ranging from young, blossoming love to those having spent an entire lifetime together. Couples of various ethnicities, couples that were pregnant, couples at the birth of their child, and couples who witnessed the loss of their spouse or child over the extended period of time that I documented various stages of their life history. I had the honor of being with a number of these couples through their peak expressions of lovemaking and through their deep moments of mourning.

We developed such a strong foundation of trust with each other as I continued to place my attention on unconditionally loving them at their core.

I interviewed each couple, asking questions about how they managed to keep their love fresh and expansive, and the recurring theme that emerged involved the practice of cultivating a deeper trust within themselves and with each other. The examples that were being demonstrated through these courageous partners left a profound imprint on my life. I was blessed to witness, time and time again, each couple's willingness to choose love over fear. I would never be the same as I witnessed firsthand the depths of union being tested through life's myriad events. By resting in the love and honoring each couple's process exactly where they were, I entered each situation as if entering the most holy of temples. As I praised their love, their wholeness and their grace, it created a living synergy of love that, in my perception, heightened their trust and connection together. Thus, the photographs reflect a true, unstaged demonstration of their devotional love and connection.

Many of the images show each couple looking into each other's eyes with such presence, and an undeniable sense of honor radiates from the photograph. Their text expresses how they continue to grow with each other and anchor in rich and fulfilling forms of self-expression and love.

Particularly poignant are the couples who have been together for over forty and fifty years. As they discuss their lifelong paths, they offer examples of how they have come to such a solid place of trust with one another. From this dedicated building of trust, they know what it looks and feels like to be fully seen by their partner. In that sacred place of being fully recognized, there is a natural out breath or exhale that occurs, a resting in the present moment with nowhere to go and nothing more important than simply being fully present, honored and seen by the other.

This most unique journey left an indelible imprint on my way of being, both in my personal relationships and professionally behind the camera. I feel 100 percent certain that when I am fully anchored in a sphere of trusting energy, the camera has the opportunity to serve as a sacred reflection of one's pure radiance, the true wholeness that cuts through all doubts, fears and preconceived notions. These precious couples taught me that through our daily devotion to telling the truth through the lens of compassion and love, we build a foundation in which it feels safe to fully be ourselves, expressing our needs and growing together like two majestic redwoods side by side. Both deep-rooted, strong and wise, sharing from the same water source, the same sunlight, and spreading our branches and our roots as we intermingle and support each other's stability throughout a long and gifted life.

Life constantly offers countless situations to practice living in a state of trust. One significant example would be the act of trusting in our beliefs. We might wish to believe that we are healthy and strong, but what about when we're tested with a real life circumstance? My neighbor Bob is in his early eighties with bright white hair and a thin, toned frame. I've always observed and admired how physically active a lifestyle Bob maintains. The man does not know the meaning of the word retirement! I often see Bob in his garage/workshop building and repairing various items. A while back, we needed some of our fence posts replaced and Bob was our man!

About two years ago, Bob's pacemaker unexpectedly stopped functioning and a helicopter flew into our mountain community and rushed him off to the nearest hospital. Did that slow Bob down? Not in the least. Shortly thereafter, I noticed Bob on the roof of his house resealing and painting around an enormous skylight. It must have needed quite a bit of repair as the ladders and scaffolding were up against the house for well over two months. Off and on, I'd see Bob up on the roof working away at his own pace.

Recently, on my daily walks past Bob's home, I noticed that there was no activity around the house and no lights were on in the evenings. A couple of weeks later, a neighbor informed me that Bob had fallen off his ladder while coming down from the roof and was taken to the hospital. When I asked his wife, Mary Jo, how Bob was coming along, she proceeded to tell me that he was in rehab and had quickly gone from being in pain to being a pain in the ass! This unexpected response brought forth great laughter and joy between us as Mary Jo continued to assure me that Bob was healing quickly and should be home soon. I asked what injuries Bob had endured and she proceeded to tell me that he had fractured both sides of his pelvis, his sacrum and his left wrist. He had also been diagnosed with blood in his brain. Sounded pretty grim for a fragile-looking man in his early eighties, right? Apparently, not from Bob's perspective.

The following week I was at our local supermarket, and in my peripheral vision, like an apparition, I saw Bob pushing the shopping cart en route out of the market. Shortly following, Mary Jo caught up with him and I walked over to greet them. He told me that he was doing well and I stood in awe as they walked to their car, Bob in shorts, his legs resembling large toothpicks, and utterly determined to carry on with his life. The following week, I was walking the dogs and approaching Bob and Mary Jo's house.

From a distance I saw someone out in the front of their home mowing the lawn. No, it couldn't be...there was Bob mowing away with a steady strength and endurance. A week later, I was driving with my wife down our country road on an early summer morning and there was Bob riding his bicycle past us, likely headed to a friend's home.

I'm always deeply inspired by examples such as Bob's. Clearly, he has such a strong, unshakeable belief that he will be healthy and strong no matter what circumstances arise. His trust in the belief that he IS a place of strength and well-being supersedes any of life's challenges that could test one's faith. It's easy to feel trusting when life's on an even keel, but our greatest opportunities to practice various forms of trust come in those difficult moments when we really need to apply it. Where in your life are you being called to go deeper in your practice of trust? What fundamental beliefs do you wish to strengthen to the degree that they are unshakeable?

Over the past few years, I've had the opportunity to work with Elton John, documenting two of his stellar shows in Las Vegas, "The Red Piano" and, more recently, "The Million Dollar Piano." Both performances proved to be outstanding in both their visual presentation and Elton's musical performance.

I recently read an interview with Sir Elton that served as a powerful example in exercising great trust with others. When he first arrived at the Colosseum at Caesar's Palace to rehearse for "The Million Dollar Piano," he had yet to see any of the staging or creative design for the show. He had such trust in the directors, Mark Fisher and Patrick Woodroffe, he gave them the list of songs and told them to simply go and do it. He didn't want

to see anything until he arrived. There was no doubt in his mind that they would come up with something amazing as they had such a solid track record of success in previously producing some of the best shows in the world. He encouraged them to go away and create from their own ideas, from Creative Director Tony King's ideas, and the input of the video team.

When Elton walked into the Colosseum for the first time and saw the staging, he was blown away with delight. People around him were surprised that he would give away such creative control, but he knew that if he was trying to influence the team's artistic expression, it would restrict their unique creative process and place a damper on what they do best. He found it most exciting in giving them a free hand to surprise him!

This story illustrates various facets in exercising trust. Because Elton had paved many years of experience in his craft, he was able to let go and trust the creative genius within his production team. Of course there was great discernment in giving free rein to these folks, as it would have been a much greater risk following such a course with a team of lesser-known success under their belts. Elton illustrates how the act of wisely trusting can open the door for being delightfully surprised and inspired.

How often are you afraid to trust what you know? Right now, you have the opportunity to make a list and take stock of what your life's experience has taught and anchored within you. Where in your life do you have the opportunity to co-create with others, and from a place of trusting discernment, allow them to perform their role fully, thus giving them the opportunity to be brilliant? In so doing, a collaborative synergy can be formed bringing greater strength, wisdom and rich wonder to the end result.

Trust in what you know…it can only bring success.

Part of living an authentic life involves our willingness to trust that it's okay to be with whatever thoughts and feelings are present in any particular moment, to honor them and give them a voice. How many times have you been in a conversation with someone and thought, I can't say THAT, because if I do, they either won't understand, they'll feel hurt, get angry, shut down, talk bad about me, leave…or a myriad of other reactions. The truth is that we live in a culture that supports our fear-based concerns. Most of us did not learn in school or from our parents the effective skills needed to communicate honestly without blaming another. Therefore, we either hold back from being fully truthful in the moment or blurt out something that's laced with blame. Making the leap into full authentic expression requires cultivating trusting that we are worthy of being heard, mixed with an unwavering faith that expressing the full truth in the long run enriches everyone.

The use of tangible tools and practices on a daily basis can serve tremendously in reminding us of our intended convictions.

Throughout the next week, I encourage you to tie a string around one of your wrists and have that string serve as a symbol, reminding you during and following every conversation you have (including with yourself), of authentically expressing the fullness of your truth. How often are you thinking, "I can't say THAT, because if I do, THIS will happen"? At the end of each day, I'd like you to journal about the day and fill in the blanks for each situation in which you held back from fully expressing yourself. How many times did you hold back from saying _____ for the fear that _____ will happen?

The more that you catch these subtle withholds, the easier it will become the next time to go deeper in trusting the value and enriching outcomes that lie before you. This is the path to living a liberated life, free from constraints, regrets and judgments.

Imagine giving this same level of attention to yourself when having your picture taken. What a marvelous reflection it can offer with each click of the shutter! "I can't express myself like THIS for fear that _____." What an amazing learning tool. If you're willing to stay open and simply observe what thoughts arise with each click, you can become more mindful and release any constricting beliefs that might be holding you back from your genuine expression. What would each frame look like if you were fully open, honest and authentic in each moment? Wow, what a liberating thought! Try it out. It will not only serve as a great learning tool, but will also offer the potential for receiving amazing photos that reveal the many dimensions of who you are.

Capturing Joy
By Kathleen McGowan

I can't look at photos of myself. I'm one of *those* people.

I pray that my children will have great memories of their childhood, because their mental images are all that they will have of me in their lives. I duck the camera every single time it is pointed at me. We have many albums of family photos, thousands of adorable pictures of smiling children on birthdays and holidays, but to look at these albums you would think that these poor babies were motherless.

It saddens me that I have let my own vanity get in the way of such important family memories, but the agony I endure when I see photos of myself has always been too great to take the risk. The camera adds ten pounds, right? Or was that twenty? I can't possibly be that heavy/that old/that red/that imperfect. So as a means of avoiding the self-flagellation that comes with viewing photos of myself, I simply refused to be photographed for as long as I could get away with it.

Man plans, God laughs.

Through God's infinite sense of humor, I landed in a career as an author and speaker that now requires me to be in front of a camera on a regular basis. While preparing my first book for international release, I knew that the inevitable "author's photograph" would have to be dealt with sooner rather than later. I didn't sleep for the three days leading up to the photo session.

The photographer chosen was an absolute professional, a compassionate and lovely woman who did everything in her power to make me feel comfortable in her studio as I attempted to pose. What do I do with my hands? Which way should my chin tilt? Who am I looking at? It doesn't help that I am a Type-A personality and terrified of making a mistake or getting it wrong. I was rigid with anxiety and trepidation, and ultimately far more focused on how sorry I was feeling for the photographer. Dealing with all of my neuroses around being photographed was clearly not an enjoyable experience for her, particularly when she had a job to do—and that was to deliver a usable head shot to a demanding publisher.

She spent many more hours with me than I am sure she had intended, and I pray that she was well paid for it. The end result was a very usable and lovely photograph—of someone I do not recognize. The overall reaction from my nearest and dearest friends was the same across the board: "It's a nice picture, but it looks nothing like you."

More grace and generosity from God led to my first book being a bestseller, and resulted in more books—and more author's photographs. And with this new wave came a new idea. My childhood best friend, the girl with whom I had shared my silliest and most cherished secrets, attended my first concerts, laughed and cried with more than any other, was back in town. And she was now one of the most accomplished celebrity and commercial photographers in the country. I hadn't seen her in a while and we had much to catch up on—our lives had taken us in very different directions—but she agreed immediately to photograph me for the new books.

We determined that the photos session would happen in my own home, which we hoped would make me more comfortable than being in a studio. My friend arrived with her team and her cameras, but before I could allow myself to get too tense, the reminiscing began. I was laughing so hard as we shared our memories that the make-up artist was having trouble getting my eyeliner on straight. But the miracle of friendship and laughter worked its magic. I was relaxed and excited to be with this old friend, and in those hours of preparation the years just slipped away. By the time she had her camera ready and pointed at me, we were kids again— young, carefree and totally comfortable with each other in our world.

In the middle of the session, my youngest son, Shane, came home from school. He was six years old at the time, and he was thrilled with all of the action happening in the house. In an impromptu moment of feeling the energy and excitement, Shane jumped up on my friend's back like a little spider monkey. We all burst into laughter and she continued to photograph me while my son played monkey on her back. For me, that moment of watching my precious child play with my oldest and dearest friend was one of such pure joy that I will never forget it. And I can't forget it, because the photograph she took of me in that moment is the shot that became my definitive author's photo.

In the most beautiful photograph of my life, I am smiling and joyous. There is a very special light on my face and in my eyes. It is a light that comes from that moment of pure joy, captured by the camera. I look at least ten years younger in that photograph—and that was without any retouching!

In addition to accomplishing the perfect image, that photo session also broke the dark spell I had been living under in terms of the camera. I no longer dread it, as I see the magic of perfect moments that can be captured by a gifted photographer.

creating a safe space

One of the primary reasons why I never get tired of taking people's portraits is because it always gives me the opportunity to create a safe space with and for them. I believe that we are all perfect and whole at our core, regardless of physical appearances. Knowing this, I love the role of reflecting this truth back to people on the other side of the camera. My intention beyond getting great photos is for people to have a direct experience of their magnificence, their beauty and their strength. Photographing people gives me the excuse *(as it's my profession)* to let my inner child out and have a ball! The truth is that I love to play, to be silly, to dance, laugh, speak in funny accents, and engage others in being playful with me. Not a bad way to "earn a living"! I'm a firm believer that we serve by example, so as I give myself permission to let go and be fully expressive, others often follow suit. Sometimes I imagine people thinking, "He must know what he's doing, right? I mean, he's photographed all these well-known people and he hasn't been booed off stage yet."

Do you recall the last time that you had your driver's license picture taken? Following is a recent experience that represents the antithesis of creating a safe space.

DMV = Detonating My Victim

If you ever wish to see one of the highest-rated dysfunctional relationships (*in my book*) related to having your picture taken, spend a couple of hours at your local Department of Motor Vehicles! I recently needed to get a new driver's license and had the pleasure of sitting, standing and squatting in this utterly soulless, fluorescent environment for two hours while waiting for my number to be called.

Throughout the first hour, I spent time meditating, sending e-mails and clearing my BlackBerry of old messages. Then I looked over my right shoulder and noticed a middle-aged female employee taking a young woman's picture for her license. I became intrigued by the setup and procedure that was being implemented, so much so that I spent the next hour studying every detail that was taking place, as if watching a lab experiment.

First, the clerk taking the picture called out a person's name. Once they approached the desk, in the most lifeless and bureaucratic tone, she slid them their license information and told them to proofread it. Once they gave the paper back to her, she commanded them to repeat their birth date and home address, I suppose to verify that they were who they said they were! Then came the fingerprinting and finally the dreaded photo instructions. In the most monotonous delivery known to man, she spoke the words, "I'll give you a 1–2–3 count, and you'll be welcome to smile." I smiled just hearing such a convincing sales pitch!

In the next hour, I witnessed people of all ages approach the camera. Most of the teens chose to frown. A number of young women put on a fashion model smile. Some people chose to grin while others looked painfully uncomfortable while forcing a tense smile. All the while, the clerk repeated her set of commands in precisely the exact same, lifeless delivery.

I began to think, "What will I choose, a smile or a grin? Neither come naturally in this sterile setting. Which look do I wish to best represent me? A smile that's more inviting or a grin that's easier to authentically bring forward? I definitely don't want an expression that's void of at least a hint of a smile as that would look too mean and unapproachable and might appear suspicious to policemen or airport security!"

"NOW SERVING NUMBER 162 AT COUNTER 5" reverberated the automated voice calling my number. I shot out of my chair, not wanting to miss my two-hour awaited appointment with the clerk at counter five. Surprisingly, the woman behind counter five talked and interacted like a real and caring person. What a wonderful reprise. She asked me a series of questions and then had me take an eye exam. I instantly became a bit alarmed as I was not expecting this to be necessary. I've never seen sharply out of my right eye and my biggest fear was that I wouldn't pass my eye test and I'd have to go through a series of useless procedures only to determine that eyeglasses would not help me see more clearly out of this eye. She asked me to place my head down into the eye viewer until my forehead pushed the viewing light on for me to begin the test. I initially didn't push hard enough and couldn't see any letters to read. Instantly, I felt a bit flustered and it took three attempts before I got the hang of it. I passed the test with flying colors and paid the clerk; then she directed me to sit down and wait for my name to be called in order to have my picture taken.

NOW SERVING NUMBER 172 AT COUNTER 5. "Just stay in your center, Carl." NOW SERVING NUMBER 173 AT COUNTER 3. "Will it be a smile or a grin?" NOW SERVING NUMBER 174 AT COUNTER 7. "Remember, Carl, nobody has power over you!" Somewhere between the automated announcements and my inner dialogue, I heard my name being called and I shot up to the counter. Only this time, I was the one going through the drill.

I reviewed all the written information, recited my date of birth and home address, laid my right index finger down on a computerized scanner *(gone are the days of ink and paper)*, stood before the camera and was told, "I'll give you a 1–2–3 count, and you'll be welcome to smile." At the final moment, I opted to grin rather than give an open-mouth smile. As much as I intended to feel relaxed and invoke a natural closed-mouth grin, I could not shake feeling nervous, self-conscious and constricted.

I was so aware of my muscles feeling tight and, if muscles could talk, they would have said, "Get me out of here! I don't want to do this. Don't force me into a position that isn't real. Why should I smile or even grin when I'm feeling afraid? This is crazy. I'll do it for you, but I just want you to know that it doesn't feel real or in integrity." The camera took the picture and the clerk took what felt like an eternity to view the image before nodding at me to leave.

I bolted out of the building into the fresh, moist Colorado air and made a beeline to my car. I sat in the car and felt like crying. I looked into the mirror only to discover that in the center of my forehead was a red indented mark. It didn't take me long to figure out that the dent was caused by my head pressing against the eye viewer during my exam. Great, not only will my driver's license picture look tense, but it will also have a red target in the middle of my forehead! Needless to say, this entire experience gave me a deeper sense of compassion for everyone that poses in front of my camera; and if I ever thought that I had risen above these concerns, I was reminded that there does exist a place to master your ability to remain centered and present in front of a camera, at your local DMV.

• • •

So, how do we cultivate an experience of feeling safe in our daily life? How do we get to the core of the part of us that's crying out for support and assurance that we are truly loved and cared for? During my morning meditations I make it a priority to connect with my inner child whom I'll call Little Carl *(L.C.)*. He is about three or four years old. I allow my "wise or higher self" to greet Little Carl with deep love and gratitude. I look into his eyes and let him know that he is such a beautiful, perfect and special little boy. I remind L.C. that he is so gifted with so many talents and that his presence in this world is such a blessing. I let him know that I am always present to support and love him. I ask L.C. if he's open to receiving a hug. He always says yes, and I wrap my arms around him and we embrace for quite a while.

As we allow ourselves to bask in the sweet exchange of love, I continue to remind him that he is always protected, even during events that feel painful and sad. I assure him that I'm always there with him, giving him love, strength and support. Sometimes he likes to climb onto my back and I take him on a series of adventures. At times we might jump from rock to rock over a running stream or climb a tree together. I rejoice in his sense of wonder and praise him as he steps out in trying something new, honoring his own pace and style of learning. By the end of our time together, Little Carl feels joy-filled, acknowledged, supported and fully loved.

This entire interaction usually takes place within five to seven minutes of my thirty-minute meditation and I find it a thoroughly effective way to anchor my day in a foundation of inner peace, trust and confidence. I am fully convinced that when our inner child feels completely safe and fully loved, our adult choices are guided with a greater clarity, ease and flow. When the doubt and fear of our inner child is no longer dominating our thoughts and feelings, we are open vessels and conduits for our greatest of expression a. our fullest of gifts to be accessed and expressed. During these times, we ar. unstoppable, for we are simply saying yes to our highest of purpose and

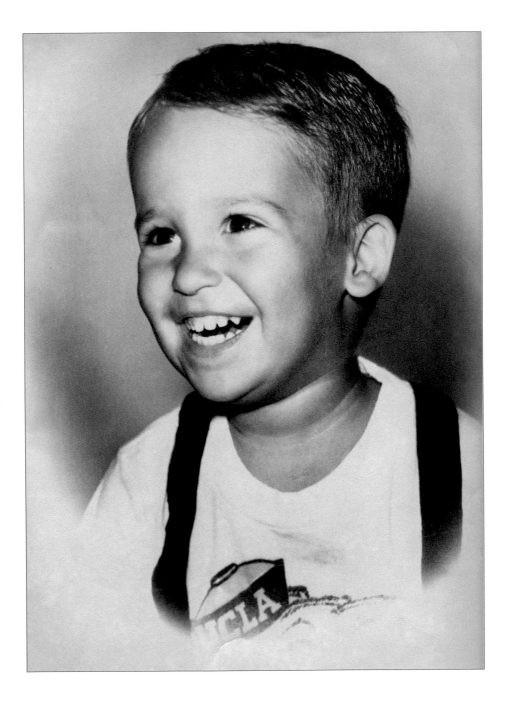

allowing our unique gifts to serve others with such tremendous value. As we radiate this unique expression, we are fully open to receiving others' gifts, for we are in a state of such receptivity, knowing our true value and worth.

In my spiritual coaching practice, I guide clients through this process and encourage them to integrate it into their daily spiritual practice. I invite you to make this practice a priority in your daily life. Most of us were not raised with this level of nurturing, this moment-to-moment feeling of being honored and praised. It's taken me many years to discover *(through countless trial and error)* that nobody else can really give this to me, not a spouse, a parent, a child, a boss, a coworker, a spiritual guide or a therapist. We must feel loved from within. We must know with certainty that at our core we are always whole, perfect and complete. Until we fully know and embody this certainty, there will always be a part of us that is searching outside ourselves for the answers, the success and the validation.

It's imperative that we create time each day in the stillness to listen and honor our needs at the core level, for if we ignore them, they will inevitably rise to the surface and demand a voice. Take this moment and make a commitment to your inner child to honor and listen to its needs daily. I assure you that if you make this a constant practice, you will begin to notice yourself feeling safer and at peace throughout each day.

what is the essential moment?

Every time that I pick up a camera, it serves as a reminder in honoring each essential moment. Whenever I click the camera's shutter, I am making a choice to document something. The question is, what will that something be and will it be of any value to others or myself? I've been shooting for so many years that I don't think about my choices each time I take a picture, as it's really become an intuitive process. I feel into the experience, meaning that something calls to me and I say yes to it. It might be the way that the warmth of the late afternoon light falls onto the backside of a golden aspen leaf causing it to become illumined amidst its more shadowed neighbors, or a brilliant blue butterfly that lands perfectly, spreading its wings and resting them in an exact pattern matching the shape of the green leaf below.

I had the opportunity to document the intimate love expressed through a beautiful couple named Ron and Priska. At one point during the day, we decided to take some pictures in a spectacular pool underneath a waterfall. I came prepared with an underwater camera, fins, a snorkel and diving mask. The couple shed their clothing and all three of us proceeded to sink beneath the pool's surface and allow mystery and magic to unfold. They began to wrap themselves around each other in various loving poses that conveyed a sacred feeling of giving and receiving *(coming up for air when needed)*.

This was before the digital age, when I was using film and I was simply trusting what I thought would turn out well. Underneath the water's surface, I could see these shimmering light patterns that were falling onto their bodies, creating interesting designs. The couple allowed themselves to tenderly express the grace, power and intimacy of their love, and I sensed that some good shots would come of it. Later, when I reviewed each frame on the proof sheet, I was overwhelmed by one particular image. My first thought was, "I didn't take this!" meaning that there was a much greater force at play orchestrating this perfect picture and it was far greater than anything that I could have possibly designed. It was truly a magnificent moment being imprinted through my camera and viewed through the form of a picture. From that time forward, I've always known that my job is to show up and allow that perfect and essential moment to be seen, be one with it and invite it home with me via the tool of my trusty camera.

How do you become finely attuned to those essential moments in your life? They're easiest to see when involved with something that inspires or ignites you.

In 1970, I was fourteen years old and my hair was rapidly growing long. One afternoon following school, I recall rushing back to my bedroom and making a beeline for my stereo record player. Clutched tightly in my hands was Paul McCartney's first solo album following The Beatles' breakup. I anxiously ripped open the plastic sealer and unfolded the double-paged album design. There was a composite of pictures taken by Paul's wife, Linda, all very personal and inviting. The back cover photo depicted a bearded Paul outdoors in the Scottish countryside in a warm winter coat, and a young baby was nestled in the garment, both looking serenely at the camera. I was instantly struck by the intimate and creative moment captured and wished I could be there with them. I placed the album on the turntable and listened with great anticipation, hoping that Paul's solo music would compare to the flawless perfection of The Beatles. I had grown up with this band from childhood to adolescent; they had served as way-showers, reminding me that being an adult could include expressing yourself creatively, having a good time, being extremely successful while offering goodness to the world. As I listened to each song, I was transported to a land of joy and safety.

Twenty-one years later, in 1991, I was driving into Skywalker Ranch in Northern California. My hair flowed halfway down my back and I intentionally hadn't shaved in days. I had been commissioned to spend two days with Sir Paul and the Industrial Light & Magic crew while shooting his "Off the Ground" video. As I entered the French chateau-style studio, an attractive young woman named Mary met me and proceeded to show me around the set. Mary asked me to follow her to the nearby trailer to meet her parents. Instantly, a light bulb flashed in my head as I recalled the iconic picture of McCartney on his first solo album. As Mary guided me to the trailer outside the studio, I had a good suspicion about whom I'd be meeting. My mind was reeling as I pieced together the connection… *"Yes, Paul and Linda's first daughter is definitely named Mary, and she IS the baby on the back cover of the album!"*

Mary guided me into the trailer where I met her parents, Paul and Linda. Out of my wildest dreams, I spent the next two days immersed in the creative world of Paul and his family while getting paid to take a wide variety of candid and posed portraits. Paul couldn't have been more kind,

whistling and singing with the crew and being quite playful in front of the camera. In fact, he appeared more comfortable in front of the camera than anyone I'd ever photographed. Completely at ease, which shouldn't be a surprise given that he's likely one of the most photographed people on the planet!

I have absolutely no doubt that the seeds of inspiration that were planted into my consciousness at age fourteen propelled me in later life to seek out this man who fed my soul and uplifted my Spirit as I grew from child to young adult. Looking back at the experience, I'm clear that my deepest calling was to creatively connect with Paul and his family and that's exactly what transpired. One referral led to the next as I was motivated by what had deep meaning for me.

I recall sitting in McCartney's manager's office in London feeling completely at ease while sharing with him about my background and holding the attitude *(in the form of a deep clarity and knowing)* that I would be a perfect match to spend time with and photograph Paul. There was no doubt in my mind or in my approach as I shared about myself and the gifts that I had to offer. We were 100 percent present while fully enjoying each other's company. I was aware of living in the "let go," in the "Yes" of each moment and allowing the "Yes-ness" to have its way! On the spot, he called Paul's publicist *(who booked all photo shoots)* and sent me over to meet with him. The same flow, ease and certainty prevailed with the publicist and within months, I was asked to document the "Off the Ground" video shoot. Throughout this period, I was fully receptive and embracing each essential moment.

What are those essential moments in your life? Are you practicing being present and open to those stellar "gems" as they appear, or are you too preoccupied with other thoughts that they just pass you by? Where is your attention right now? Is it focused in the future in wanting to get somewhere, or perhaps in the past dwelling on some old regret or judgment? If our attention tends to waver away from honoring the present moment, how can we fully see and experience the richness of the gifts at hand right now? What is it costing you to not be fully present to life's grand adventure in each moment? Boredom, apathy, confusion, sadness and resentment could be a few symptoms that rear their head when we're not fully listening and honoring our deepest calling.

In September of 1999, my wife Cynthia and I had the opportunity to be a part of the Synthesis Dialogues in Dharamsala, India with the Dalai Lama. Along with a host of world visionaries, I was invited to attend and document this five-day conference, which focused on exploring new paradigms for peace as we entered the new millennium. Cynthia had the role of being a witness and sharing her perspective at given moments. It was truly a life-changing experience spending five days in close quarters with His Holiness.

On the first day when the Dalai Lama was arriving, I situated myself *(with camera in tow)* on the path he'd be walking en route to the temple where the meetings were being held. As he came strolling up the path with his dear friend Brother Wayne Teasdale, I prepared myself to catch the essential moments about to unfold. What I didn't anticipate was his response to seeing me.

Before I lifted the camera to photograph, our eyes met one another's and His Holiness gave me a bright and lively smile. He proceeded to walk over to me with his hands in a prayerful position, bowing and honoring my presence. He greeted me like seeing a long-lost friend, and I continued to smile, bow my head in return and somehow simultaneously take a picture of him while in a beaming and prayerful greeting. Granted, it wasn't the sharpest picture in the world, but it served as an example of allowing all of the essential moments to be felt and expressed. Somehow, I was able to be fully present with him while taking a beautiful photograph that exemplified his radiant spirit.

Throughout the five meeting days, I was so taken by how fully present the Dalai Lama was with every single person he spoke with in these dialogues. His eyes never wavered in any form of distraction. He truly embodied being 100 percent available and devoted to each participant. I watched him seamlessly shift in speaking from the wise sage perspective to a complete *(laughing)* childlike nature, always being with each person exemplifying utmost compassion and honor. My life has not been the same since this experience. The Dalai Lama serves as a living example of a human being who lives compassion and authenticity from moment to moment. I witnessed a role model who has shown me what it looks and feels like to live life from this level of honoring each present moment and honestly responding to each situation with love as it presents itself.

One day, while taking my dogs on our daily walk down our remote dirt road, the wind suddenly picked up and the sun was hidden by gray rain clouds. Suddenly, my dog Easter perked up. Her body became erect, her tail darted outward and all of her attention was riveted to my right. I looked over in the direction of her attention and barely noticed a small gray fox lying on a gray rock not much larger than her body. The fox was completely still and did not waver as we walked by.

I'm certain that I would have never noticed this pristine creature if Easter hadn't pointed her out, as she blended perfectly with the rock. For a split moment I questioned, "Should I go back and get my camera?" I'm not fully clear why I didn't act on this impulse. I do know that two thoughts passed through my awareness in answer to my question. The first was the rational thought, "No, she likely won't be there on my return," and the second was more of an intuitive directive telling me to just bask in the perfection of the moment. I'm grateful that I continued walking, for in doing so it allowed the sense of pure grace to fill me. There was nothing that interrupted that perfect moment. It felt like I was viewing an apparition, akin to being visited by an animal totem from another world, perhaps a guide that was there to offer me an illuminating realization. As I walked on, deep emotions welled up from within and I experienced truly feeling at one with everything around me.

In that split second of choice point, I listened and allowed the moment to be fully honored by not interrupting nature's perfect rhythm due to a habitual thought. As a result of trusting my inner guidance, I was able to experience a deeply mystical moment of oneness mixed with immense gratitude. Sure, I had passing thoughts of missing the opportunity to potentially document a most stunning image, but a greater part of me knew that the transcendent moment I shared with the fox and with the natural world was far more valuable than entertaining this question. I'm deeply grateful that I did not allow my egoist desires to disrupt a perfect moment.

What opportunities are present in your daily life to practice listening from your inner directive rather than from being a slave to your conditioned ego response? How willing are you to be mindful throughout your day and catch yourself every time that a fear-based, conditioned response arises? You might have thoughts of being unworthy, feeling like the world just doesn't "get" you. Or perhaps you're given a wonderful opportunity, but choose not to act on it for fear of failure.

There is always a moment of choice when we are able to decide what thoughts are valid and which are not true and do not serve our highest good. I like to imagine wearing a catcher's mitt and being alert enough to see the thought *(whether it be a judgment or any limiting idea)* flying through the air. I've got my hands in position and I'm tracking where that thought is going to land. I move into position and WHAM, a perfect catch. Once I've caught the thought, I assess the belief and if it doesn't serve me, I release it and return to the present moment's inner guidance, to the gifts that lay before me, to the inspired path that's always directing us when we remain open and receptive.

Each moment is significantly different from the next, so when you're in front of a camera in a portrait session, every frame displays the changing moment. What a great metaphor for life, being reminded of how radically different every moment is when you view frame-by-frame pictures of yourself. There might be certain frames that look similar, but if you study them closely, you'll see that your facial muscles are always shifting. Some frames might display your mouth muscles looking relaxed while your brow is a bit furled. The next picture might show your eyes resting in a soft and present focus while the next might look starry eyed.

Imagine having your picture taken and every time that a distractive thought entered into your consciousness, you "caught" it and released it almost instantly. Allowing this to be a game that you perfect, imagine the distractive thoughts coming and going so quickly that you begin to witness more and more moments of resting in the let go, in the grace of surrender where you simply are present frame by frame. Living and expressing from this purview, you find that you are living, being and breathing the essential moment, and authentic thought and feeling guide each millisecond of choice.

Now the game becomes fun and exhilarating as you begin to master what form of expression wishes to communicate in each passing moment. Imagine how fluid and inspiring it is having the complete freedom to speak to the camera through your eyes, your mouth or your body, being fully spontaneous with whatever wishes to be communicated from frame to frame. One moment you might tap into ecstatic joy, while the next deep compassion, while the next great sorrow.

In the Silence

By Cynthia James

I always knew that I wanted to be an actress. As a child, constant excitement ran through me when watching movie stars and stage performers and I would affirm, "I can do that!" I lived very close to my twelve cousins and would often assure them that I was going to be a famous singer and actor. Of course, they thought that I was just a big dreamer. Somehow, that didn't matter because I knew I was destined to share my gifts. I would often take the lead in creating family shows and we would invite our parents to view our incredible talents. As I look back on that time, it was a period of such freedom, as I always felt overjoyed to sing, dance and tell stories. I do not ever remember feeling self-conscious.

While living in Los Angeles and making my living as an actress and singer, I was drawn to discover a deeper knowledge of my gifts as a performer. I was very interested in becoming more authentic and powerful as an actress, having studied with wonderful teachers, including the renowned Stella Adler. However, I was clear that I hadn't yet tapped into the well that made me great at my craft.

One day, I saw an ad in an entertainment magazine. It was an invitation to study with Tad Danielewski, who was beginning a master class for professional actors. Tad had studied at the Royal Academy of Dramatic Arts in London and started the Professional Actors Workshop in New York City, whose students included Martin Sheen, James Earl Jones and Mercedes Ruehl. His background was amazing. Something about the ad spoke to me and I knew I was meant to study with this man.

I later found out that he was born in Poland, served in the Polish underground during World War II and eventually ended up in a concentration camp. Why is this important? Because his past had taught him to treasure every moment, and this reminder was one of the many gifts he brought to being an acting teacher.

The first night was very intimidating. The high level of actors in the class was amazing. They were proficient, powerful and very clear about their talents. I must say that I was not living in that level of awareness at the time.

Tad was an extraordinary teacher. One of the great gifts he gave me, besides his friendship, was calling forth and acting from your most authentic experience. When we began working on challenging scenes, to our surprise, a camera was in the room when we arrived. Tad told us that we were to be taped and then we would review the tapes after the scene work. We were all accustomed to being in front of cameras, so this did not seem out of the ordinary.

After the scene work, we sat together with Tad before us. He shared that we were going to watch the scenes without sound. Needless to say, there was a little resistance. Questions flew into the room. "Why are we doing that?" "How can we get the full meaning without the words?" and "How will you know if we fulfilled the point of the scene?" Tad smiled gently and said, "Everything that needs to be said and understood can be experienced in the silence." I was intrigued with the prospect and was willing to take the ride.

What occurred that evening changed me forever, as an actor and as a person. In scene after scene, we witnessed moments of deep connection and brilliance. We also saw moments of trying too hard, pushing energy, phoning in the performance, and fear overtaking the actor's ability to be present. It was stunning. At the end, we were speechless. Tad shared his message that the gift is in the silence.

True magic is created within the heart and soul of the actor in those moments where we choose to be fearless, present and tell the truth. The words are the icing on the cake. He invited us to view television shows, movies, political speeches and commentaries. We were told that we could always see authenticity, or lack thereof, if we turned down the sound.

My mind raced as I thought of the possibilities of turning down my "inner sound," that critical voice that needed to be loved, seen, validated and acknowledged. I remember thinking, "What if the mere act of turning off those incessant voices of need could create genius in my work and in my life?" I began to experiment with becoming more present in each moment and trusting that the authenticity of the character would emerge through me if I got out of my own way. Miraculous things occurred. I was getting roles and working in ways that were deeper and richer than ever before.

But here is the grand news: my life was changing. I began to sing through my heart, speak from places of love and clarity and step through portals of fearless living. It was transformative and exhilarating. I began experiencing the childlike joy of sharing my gifts and shining my light. It was time to make sure that every aspect of my life reflected this new awakening.

After my experience with Tad, I wanted to get new actor's headshots that represented my expanded awareness. I have always felt open and naturally comfortable in front of cameras, especially still photography shoots for publicity and actor's headshots. Having never understood people's fear of being in front of a camera, I've always been excited to see the product of a creative shoot and love how relaxed I feel. I believe that photographs are the entrée that allows others to see the truth of who we are. Casting directors, film directors and agents often decide whether they want to meet you based on your photo. I discovered that most photographers are not intentional about cap-turing your authentic essence. They want beautiful pictures, but that does not always mean that your inner beauty will come through.

When I first met Carl and asked him to take new photos of me, I was not aware of his "true" gift. I was clear that I was going to bring my essence to the session and hoped it would be captured. I quickly realized that Carl wanted me to have that experience as well.

As the shoot began, I connected to the stillness within me and invited it to be present. I actively decided to be authentic in each moment and allow my true self to come forward. At the same time, Carl was using his skill to bring forth my essence. As a result, I received a heart-opening experience and an unexpected gift. I could actually see my soul coming through my eyes. My agents and friends were telling me, "These are the best pictures we've seen of you." I was clear that my desire to be present was being realized and met through the gifted talent of one who was dedicated to bringing forth and sharing the light in each person.

Today, as an author, speaker, singer/composer and teacher, the practice of moving into the silence is an integral component in my preparation for any event or class. That can take the form of meditation, contemplation, walking in nature or journaling. I practice with the intention of sharing in a way that can be heard and fully experienced in the heart of the recipient. I do not care about the size of the audience. I care about the interconnectedness and communication that takes place within each soul.

At the completion of each presentation, the only question I ask myself is, "If each person before me had turned off the sound…would they have heard and felt the heart and reality of this message?" If the answer is yes, I am satisfied. If the answer is no…I go back to my inner work and clear out any remnants of need. My deepest desire is to allow the beautiful child within me to fulfill her first calling; to express fully. She is a constant reminder that I am here to shine my light.

now you see it, now you don't

How often are you holding onto a particular thought, opinion or perception as fact, only to have it later change? Has the actual circumstance altered or is it your perception that has shifted? Quantum physics now tells us that the observer of an experiment can, and often does, change the results due to their beliefs in what the outcome will be. In other words, if our thoughts are held with a consistently strong conviction, they will help mold the outcome of our physical experience.

Let's apply this principle to how we see ourselves when reviewing pictures taken of us. As we continue to live a longer life with a wider selection of pictures taken throughout the years, our perception of ourselves continues to broaden. Meaning, as we become wiser and more attuned to various subtleties of behavior, we're able to distinguish greater dimensions in past pictures of ourselves. This could include how confident *(or not)* we look through posture and facial expressions, choices in clothing, people that we chose to spend time with, activities that we were involved in, how happy or sad that we appear and what our priorities were.

You may ask yourself, "How do I choose to view photographs of myself? Am I looking from a critical and judgmental purview, or am I seeing them as a fascinating tool for learning

Photographs truly serve as a time capsule in documenting many of the multidimensional aspects of our life history.

more about myself?" These golden road maps have the opportunity to offer deep insights, yet most of us close the door on these precious gems when our self-judgment surfaces. We've become so conditioned in immediately labeling photos as either flattering or unflattering, and if they're the latter, we wish to rip them up or delete them as quickly as humanly possible.

Here's a great exercise that will serve you well if you choose to participate. From this moment forward, every time that you view a picture of yourself that you like or despise *(or anywhere in between)*, stop and ask yourself, "What is it about this image that evokes the feeling and decision that I'm making? What can this image teach me about myself, or what is there to learn from this picture?" When we release our attachment to how we think we should look, act or be, we are free to simply observe and to benefit from the understanding that surfaces from this exploration.

I recently spent several days with my eighty-eight-year-old father. At one point, he shared with me a group picture from a recent family wedding of all the grandparents present taken with the bride and groom. As I viewed the photo, *(from my professional assessment)* it looked as if the picture had been taken between expressions. My father was looking slightly away from the camera with a serious or sullen look on his face. After viewing, I expressed this perspective to him and told him that I didn't think it was a great shot.

Several hours later following a discussion with Dad about being one's authentic self in front of a camera, he turned to me and said, "I was being myself in that picture I showed you and you were suggesting that I smile. Isn't that contradictory to your message?"

At first, I became a bit defensive in explaining that I felt he was in between expressions and that the pose was not a flattering one. He responded by saying, "No, I don't agree, that's really me. That's how I see myself and I like the picture! When I smile for the camera, I'm not being real, whereas this is really me." Well, how could I disagree with him? My own father caught me in a conditioned thought.

The truth is that there are times that I take pictures of him and *(I'm pretty certain)* get an authentic smile, and the rest of the time he likely puts on a conditioned smile for the camera. In my eyes, the picture we were discussing did not look natural or flattering, but who am I to disagree with someone who likes or identifies with a particular expression or pose of themselves? How much of my perception was being clouded by the notion that I like to see my dad looking happy and upbeat? Perhaps if I restudied that particular photo, I might learn more about my father in how he sees and identifies himself in the world. Perhaps there's a deeper layer of contemplation and feeling that is being reflected through this image, beyond the veneer of a conditioned, happy-go-lucky smile?

In the late eighties, I had the honor of doing a photo session with the gifted teacher Ram Dass. Weeks before the scheduled shoot, my dear friend Jacquelyn Holley Pogue interviewed Ram Dass, with each question focused on discussing his inner life. Jacquelyn and I had come up with the idea of designing an interview that would shed insights into this wise man's most valued choices and perceptions related to how he sees himself and how he views the world. From this interview, I took specific symbols and references to create a series of portraits that reflect his values and what he'd most like to see in a portrait of himself that would serve as a tool for growth and for self-awareness. Below is this interview coupled with several matching portraits.

Interview with Ram Dass

Tell me about your inner life?

The deepest thing in my life is my relationship with my guru, Neem Karoli Baba, and that's a dialogue that continues unabated. It includes everything: making love, working in developing countries, having kidney stones, cleaning out the garbage, and all else. It's about having a dialogue with God all of the time. I disappear into the moment, and that quality offers such fullness and richness. I guess that it's always been rich, but I just didn't notice it when I was so busy focusing on the past and the future. That richness has in it a sense of grace, appreciation, reverence, joy and love. All those things are relevant to the moment. And even in this moment when I am physically sick and tired, I am still graceful. I'm learning how to live with a lot of emptiness, not in the negative sense, but in the sense that nothing is. It's what spiritual beings call the living dead. They have died to the world and then they go on. In a way, I have died a lot to the world. I am not dead, but I am dying. I don't seem to have the need to make drama exist.

What happens without the drama?

New qualities appear related to integration and integrity, growing into all the aspects of your being. This is especially relevant when you realize that your being includes everything, so there is a lot of surrendering into the various parts of yourself. While one part is dying, another part is cuddling in bed, another part wants to play with a mind thought, while another part is brokenhearted about the suffering. I have stopped measuring and counting; I don't know where it all goes. It's just an unfolding process, a process full of wonder.

How does this relate to your everyday life?

I've got more power in the worldly sense of getting what I want than I have ever had in my life, and yet there is less that I want. So I am faced with this predicament that there's nothing to do once I get here, which makes it very exciting. I think I live with Gandhi's statement, "My life is my message." I feel I have to be what I talk about. I have to be very truthful. I'm kind of amazed and delighted at how beautiful I turned out to be. I didn't ever really think I'd be beautiful, I mean on the inside. For most of my life I didn't really feel this beauty.

What would serve you in remembering that beauty that you now recognize? What would touch your heart and keep it open and surrendered to the growing place of oneness?

While I was in Jaipur, India, I was helping an artist do the sketches of Hanuman, the monkey that ended up being the murti that is in New Mexico. I said to the artist, "Make it so that every time you look at it, you feel it's your child, and your father, and your lover and your friend." It reminds me of the king who threatened to destroy a people. He told them that if they could devise a way to make him happy when feeling sad, they would be saved. So they designed a ring for him that read, "And this too shall pass away." There's a cartoon of my guru and me in which he is the organ grinder and I'm the monkey on the string with a cup. It's delicious. It's a beautiful cartoon. In a way, every time I see it, it reminds me that I'm just a pawn in the game, and I love it.

Aside from your relationships, who are you?

I had an interesting experience once. Timothy Leary and I went to a party in New York. We were going to be on an all-night radio talk show called, *The Long John Neville Show*. We took acid on the way and I received the part of the sugar cube that was the most concentrated. There was a girl sketching famous (*and not-so-famous*) people and she asked if she could sketch me. As she began, I thought, "Who am I? I am a young man, a teacher." But I didn't move; I just thought it and she took the gum and erased her sketching. Then I thought of something else again, and she took out her eraser once more. Eventually, after thinking several new thoughts related to who I was, she finally said, "I can't draw you." In a way, this external form isn't who I am, to the degree that it's almost irrelevant. In a way, the absence of the form is almost the form because who I am is certainly not my age. I'm a baby and I'm an old man. It's interesting because if I see who I am through the projections of other people, it takes me off track as they have nothing to do with the experience I have of myself. There are so many levels of me—a very middle-class person who loves nature and softness and quiet and ease and beauty, and yet there's another part of me that's very much at home in Calcutta or any heavy-duty environment.

What symbols reflect different parts of yourself?
The eyes of the Buddha from the Swayambhunath Temple that are the Seva Logo. That is an important symbol in my life; those eyes represent enlightenment. Hanuman is also important because it is my lineage and is another name for Ram Dass, meaning "servant of God. "

Are your eyes a focus for spiritual expression?
Yes, along with my hands and heart, but the strongest part of the message comes from my eyes and voice. In a film about Mother Teresa, there's a scene where the nurses are working with a spastic child. They are putting their hands on the young girl and their hands are so frankly compassionate. I spend a lot of time hugging people, and when I hug, I really experience slowing them down until they know they exist for a moment. There's a very beautiful picture of me hugging Stephen Levine at the beginning of a videotape; we're just delightful.

When you are being photographed, what kinds of responses do you have?
I'm vulnerable to my relational needs. I really become who that photographer wants me to be. I take very different photographs with each one. Often when I'm being photographed, I feel that the photographer doesn't really touch me. The photographer is focused on what his camera is seeing. Although, in some really great photographers, I see the spirit comes through the photograph.

If your spirit could be glimpsed through a photograph, what would be portrayed?

I can imagine a photograph in black and white where it is so contrasting that it looks as if it's starting to disappear into nothing—a picture that looks underdeveloped or is starting to fade. A highly focused photograph doesn't feel like what I am. I'm not sure that a picture of me as a skeleton might not be most useful, or a picture of me taken through a prism showing all the different ways it splits into so many things. Or even something that shows the humor of the predicament of existence. Something the photograph should also do is ground me, bust me or keep me human. It would probably show me angry or uptight or perverse or devious or manipulative.

How do photographs serve to inspire you?

I have hundreds of photographs of my guru and many have facial expressions that affect me in different ways. I have a huge photo that I work with most of the time. He's looking beyond, and yet he sees nothing special. There's a humor and a lightness that's present. Each image has its own message, and at times my mind is drawn to one or another. Though the pictures are important to me, they are less important all the time because he is not the picture.

i can imagine a photograph in black and white where
it is so contrasting that it looks as if it's starting
to disappear into nothing, a picture that looks
underdeveloped or is starting to fade

something the photograph should also do is ground me,
bust me or keep me human. it would probably show me
angry or uptight or perverse or devious or manipulative

*something that shows the humor
of the predicament of existence*

along with my hands and heart the strongest part
of the message comes from my eyes and voice

is being self-conscious a bad thing?

The interesting thing to me about the term "self-conscious" is that when you take it apart, it simply means to be conscious of one's self. In a literal translation, I would define that as being aware of one's way of thinking, speaking, acting and overall way of being. Bringing a greater sense of awareness to our self is a good thing, right?

How did this expression take on such a bad rap? I grew up with people telling me, "Don't be so self-conscious." I began to interpret that as meaning, "Don't become overly aware of every action you do and every thought that you think as it will cause you to become tentative and insecure in your way of being in the world." It's fascinating how a truly virtuous expression has become tainted with an interpretation of being insecure and unsure of oneself.

How can one be overly aware? No can do! Just for the record, I say, "Be self-conscious...be very self-conscious!" The greater that we bring consciousness to every area of our Selves, the wiser that we become. Since consciousness is the same as truth, "The truth shall set you free." Perhaps it's time for us to use more accurate words to define what we've been calling self-consciousness. Words like overly self-critical, overly analyzing, questioning to the degree of bringing on angst and un-surety. Perhaps it's time to bring a greater sense of self-consciousness to these areas of our lives that are in dire need of light and truth.

I have found no greater, more effective way to integrate self-conscious awareness into my life than through a daily practice of meditation. In 1973, I was seventeen years old and my girlfriend Ina expressed interest in becoming initiated into Transcendental Meditation. She asked me to join her in this ritual and I said yes.

Looking back, I'm clear that one of the primary reasons why I felt called to jump into these unknown waters was due to The Beatles' influence. In 1968, the "fab four" traveled to India to spend time with the Maharishi Yogi, practicing Transcendental Meditation and deepening in their spiritual awareness. Given that I was a huge Beatles fan and trusted their choices, I felt safe to explore this unknown realm called meditation. As part of our initiation, both Ina and I were given our own secret mantras and we learned how to practice reciting this word silently as a way of canceling out all thoughts and outward distractions. We agreed to make this practice a daily ritual and we did keep it up for several months.

One day after school, we were at a mutual friend's house and we excused ourselves, found the most private place in the house *(which happened to be a closet off the main hallway)*, and devotedly practiced our meditation. We sat cross-legged on the closet floor, allowed our eyes to close and began our process. In the midst of our deepening stillness, the closet door opened as did our eyes, and we saw the feet of our friend's mother as she hovered over us. When we told her that we were meditating, that concept was so far out of her awareness that she couldn't begin to comprehend what we were talking about. I'm certain that in her purview, we were in the closet for the most obvious reason that any healthy, teenage couple would be…to make out!

Looking back, I'm clear that learning the practice of meditation at such a young age opened within me a door to recognize what it feels like when I'm not distracted by my constant mind chatter. Meditation serves as a touchstone for deepening my self-awareness. It serves as a reminder that I always have a tool that will assist me in traveling to that still place where clarity naturally resides. It has taught me that the mind is not my source for gaining guidance and wisdom. Therefore, while maturing into adult life and up to this present moment, I've always had an anchor to rest upon when my mind hasn't been able to come up with the answers *(which is most of the time!)*. There were many years that my meditation practice was sporadic, but for the past several, I've made it a priority to meditate daily, and it's now become such an anchored habit that I wouldn't consider starting the day without it.

I had the honor of spending an hour over tea with George and Olivia Harrison in 1992 when I was photographing George's historic three-week tour of Japan. This was a scenario out of my wildest dreams as George was the primary influence in bringing The Beatles to India to anchor in Transcendental Meditation. As I sat with this beaming figure of a man, we primarily discussed the importance of maintaining a solid, daily spiritual practice. George spoke of a recent time in his life when he neglected his daily meditation practice. During this period, he found

himself reverting back to certain old habits such as smoking, habits that clearly did not support his health or his well-being. Once he resumed his daily practice, he found that his life choices were grounded in a deeper sense of self-honoring and a grander sense of wellness washed over him.

It was truly a blessing to share this poignant conversation with the very man who served as my primary influence at age seventeen as I was testing the waters of this unchartered territory known as meditation. I could not have received a more powerful reminder, a more potent wake-up call than to hear it from the source influence himself! If I ever start to question whether to begin the day in stillness via meditation, I have this vivid memory to call me back to center.

Meditation serves in shifting our attention from the outer conditions of life to the inner stillness and guidance that is ever-present, residing at the core of each of our beings. As we become accustomed to listening and being directed from this still point, confusion, judgment, the need to figure things out and the appearance of separation fall by the wayside and a deeper cultivation of "Self Consciousness" is rooted in our daily experience.

When I'm in the act of taking someone's portrait, I see them in their perfection, beyond their own doubts and fears. Both silently and verbally, I praise and recognize the wholeness of the individual who stands before me. I call myself "The Affirminator," and I use each defining moment as a time of canceling out any untruths about them. I smile, I laugh, I dance, I speak in silly accents, and I remind them that this is the best moment of their life. If my energy is too bold, I tone it down and speak with a softer and more tranquil composure. I listen to the needs of the individual from that still, intuitive center and fully honor who they are at their essence.

See and Be Seen

By Leilani Raashida Henry

I'm curious why some people easily embrace being in front of a camera, while others have absolutely no desire to be captured in a photo. When I have my picture taken, it's usually an opportunity to project myself outward and it feels as natural as smiling at a friend. My family reports that from birth I responded to the camera as a playful toy. Perhaps it's a love of interaction. I think of it as sending love through a box as it captures a moment like nothing else. On a recent trip to Hawaii, I heard a number of people mention how dolphins enjoy having their picture taken, how they often seem to pose and wait until you are ready, giving you the perfect shot!

My relationship with the camera is one of curiosity. I wonder, "What does the camera see that I don't?" I love the immediate feedback from the camera that shows me my everyday expressions. I see how subtle facial movements look to other people. I also see what I didn't intend to portray with my body. It's a great mirror that allows me to examine if my inner thoughts and feelings are congruent with what another is noticing.

There are moments when I imagine I look my worst, and a picture gives me the relief to find that I don't look as bad as the image in my mind's eye. The reverse can happen as well, when I view a photo and notice a blemish or a line on my face that I didn't realize was there. Waves of disappointment surface and I tend to reinforce the doubts I face. I think, "You are not pretty enough! Who do you think YOU are in wanting to look so good? Who cares about how you look?"

Pictures can reflect back to me my true positive self, a window into my soul that I can feel but can't see when looking in a mirror. Magic happens when the photographer sees who I am at my core. Though I'm usually comfortable in front of the camera, I had an experience that stretched my comfort zone. A couple years ago, I hired a notable international photographer. I dreamed of doing a shoot with him because of his talent in bringing out the best in his subjects.

It's a beautiful sunny day in the Rocky Mountains and I feel a bit nervous about whether I will get pictures that I like. Frequently, I enjoy my looks, though there are times when I find it difficult to look at myself. The exercise of a photo shoot offers me the opportunity to get real with who I am, what I look like and to accept things I cannot change, which in this case is my looks!

I am concerned that my outfits are not quite right. The pressure I feel keeps building. It's not enough that I have to *worry* about my face. I can't figure out the look I want—not too corporate, but professional and competent. The stakes seem high! I don't feel ready and time is running out. I pull together a red tank top and suit with a gorgeous swing jacket. Makeup and hair are as perfect as they can be. We begin the shoot. The photographer helps me to relax by asking questions, smiling and finding various flattering angles.

I am recently certified in Matrix Energetics®. My energy is very high. This practice encourages me to imagine a place that is whole, complete and positive. It provides a freedom to explore various dimensions of light, color and energy while bringing them into the present moment. Therefore, it creates a sense of excitement that taps into one's highest intentions.

Suddenly, I am sharing stories from the Matrix workshop, explaining the crazy things Dr. Richard Bartlett did to teach us that anything is possible. "Just play with the matrix. Everything is energy and information and we get to choose how we want things to be." In that moment, I forget about the high stakes and simply sink into myself. That's the key. The pictures are stunning. Usually, out of a hundred pictures, I might get four or five that I can use, but in this case, I have plenty more to choose from.

This photo session taught me that when intentional energy flows, the photographer and the camera see things we normally don't see. My intention was to bring out a different side of myself and to use this exercise as a way of stretching my comfort zone. My desire was to let the camera help me step into my power and be seen by others in a new way.

Viewing the pictures, I saw an outgoing, confident person, ready to thrive! We created such a positive, energetic experience that it took several months before I integrated the new me into my promo materials. Until this point, I saw myself as a more reserved, introverted person. Being fully seen was a challenge for me. That's the key. When we allow ourselves to be fully seen, we more easily receive affirmations and positive reinforcement from others. When we receive, we also increase our ability to give our light to others and allow them to shine as well!

I saw new possibilities in those pictures! Seeing my expressions, which a mirror will not reflect, is one of the greatest gifts that I've received. The communication is beyond words; the simple shift of an angle from homely to pretty is truly a joy!

releasing judgment and opening to the broader picture

What if there was no one or nothing to compare yourself to? How would you feel about yourself in each moment? Where would your attention be? Well, this was certainly not the cultivated awareness throughout my formative years of growing up. At times, I think about how my life would have been vastly different had I attended a school that honored the unique pace and preferences of every student. What a concept! I witness some of my friends' children who attend Waldorf schools and see a level of freedom and self-assurance that simply seems to breathe through them. They are being raised, both in school and in the home environment with a consistent level of honoring the uniqueness at their core. I think about how differently my childhood would have been had I received this level of acceptance for my pace and way of learning. I wish I had a nickel for every time I was told that I wasn't doing something right or fast enough. I'd be a very rich man!

I personally believe that if we didn't experience constant criticism as children, we would not have such an instant tendency to judge ourselves (*and thus judge others*) throughout each day. On the other hand, because I felt such a victim to criticism, laughter and exclusion, this sensitivity birthed a deep level of compassion for others and the human condition.

Judgments can also filter into our awareness in the most subtle ways, not just toward an individual, but in our assessment of the world around us. I was driving through the mountains of Colorado and noticed in certain regions that a large percentage of the pine trees were dying. I learned that due to climate change along with other ecological factors, specific pines were more prone to beetle infestation. Due to warmer winters, there has not been the level of frost needed that generally kills a percentage of these insects. Plus, the trees have been under greater stress due to less moisture causing them to be greater targets for these beetles.

My first response was one of deep sadness and regret. My next response was one of anger, fueled by a subtle form of judgment. Once I stopped and truly examined the belief, I could see that I was judging humanity for being greedy and not in touch with how our choices have brought us to experiencing the repercussion of climate change. I held onto this judgment for quite a while, simply feeling bad and helpless over this condition.

Recently, I was driving to a beautiful Colorado mountain community where I regularly teach a nature photography class. I hadn't been to this location in two years and, as I drove up the mountain, I began to see more and more lodgepole pines that were dying. As I entered the park where my class would take place, I was stunned at how many trees had died within the last two years! I did not recall any trees looking at risk the last time I'd been there.

I drove to my cabin and could not help but notice that when looking forward with my back to the front of the cabin, all I could see were these once beautiful, older majestic trees in a rapid state of decay. I walked into my cabin, peered out the back window and was stunned as I viewed an area of

the park that had been affected by fire fifteen years earlier and could see a lush, new grove of pines and aspens sprouting vibrantly. Two years earlier, this area did not look nearly as lush or grown in.

In that moment, as I was given such a graceful reminder of nature's path of evolution, I felt a spark of insight. I realized that when viewing through our human perception of time, all I could see were the dying trees and how ugly and sparse the landscape appeared. I was viewing through my esthetic purview of what I perceive as being beautiful. Yet, from a grander view of time, nature is always having things die and be reborn as witnessed by this vital and lush new grove of trees.

When I released my judgment over the situation, I could see a much grander scheme at play that not only made a lot of sense, but also felt quite reassuring. Nature will always find its perfect equilibrium regardless of humanity's influence or involvement. When we're able to release our judgments, we're able to see the larger truth that lies before us.

The trick is how to recognize judgment as it surfaces so that we can then diffuse it with the light of love. I've come to recognize that all judgment, whether toward others or myself, has a dissonant tone or vibration attached to the thought that's entering my consciousness. What do I mean by that?

Imagine being in the most peaceful, safe and nurturing of places. It could be a beautiful, spring mountaintop or a tropical beach filling you with radiant sunshine. Feel the stillness and grace that fills your entire being with a deep sense of freedom, letting go to the essence of love. Notice how naturally you are breathing full, life-affirming breaths. You feel fully safe, warm and protected without a care in the world. Sense how that feels in your body and in your field of energy. Now think of a person who has treated you with disrespect and dishonored your feelings to the point that you've felt hurt or angry. How has this thought changed your inner landscape? Are you now experiencing a shallower breathing pattern? Is your heart beating a bit faster? Are you feeling the need to protect yourself? Is there a certain level of tension that now exists in your body and in your thoughts, perhaps a certain degree of separation that you are now feeling from others and the world around you?

I imagine that throughout this exercise it was fairly simple to recognize the vast difference in how you felt from the peace-filled scenario to the one of agitation. The art is in learning to recognize this difference in energy when a judgment passes through your moment-to-moment awareness. Consider that anytime you shift from a peaceful state of being to one of agitation or separation there is a judgment involved! The only exception would be if you are physically threatened in one form or another and, in this case, it's a natural response to protect ourselves.

So how do you sharpen your ability to immediately see a judgment as it surfaces? I've found that it's often easier to see the feeling behind a judgment before I'm even aware of the thought that's surfaced. If you look back at the above exercise, you likely found it fairly simple to notice a difference in how you felt once you were feeling judged or criticized. The more you become attuned to what it feels like to be at peace with each breath and each thought, the more obvious it will become when you're not feeling peaceful or harmonious.

There are times that I'll stop myself and think, "What just happened? A moment ago I was feeling open and at peace, and now I'm feeling worried and uneasy." Just being able to catch that shift in feelings allows me to then track what thoughts recently entered my awareness that brought me down. I always find that those thoughts are related to a judgment toward myself *(often questioning my self-worth)* or directed at someone else in the form of blame. Once I recognize the judgment, I make it a priority to take time out *(when feasibly possible)* and bring loving forgiveness to the judgment. I recognize what the judgment is and then forgive myself for judging someone or most often myself for that judgment. This always seems to neutralize the energy and bring me back to a place of tranquility.

Imagine how you'd respond when having your picture taken if there were no judgments present. I imagine you'd show up in front of the camera and simply be who you are. Without any self-criticism, wouldn't you just show up radiating your authentic self?

When someone is taking my picture and they ask me to smile, I'm very aware of how unnatural it is to "try" and smile. This is one reason why so many of us feel awkward in front of a camera. I'm getting much better at letting the person behind the camera know that if they want me to smile, they need to evoke a natural smile from me, otherwise it will feel forced. Sometimes, especially with people who know me well, this instruction will give them the freedom to explore how to bring forward a natural smile from their subjects.

I love it when I witness the person with the camera begin to lighten up and be silly, or instruct their subjects to shout out an affirmative quality like YES or LOVE, thus evoking enthusiasm. The process then becomes a cooperative exchange rather than someone telling me what to do! One of the reasons why I'm able to be clear with the picture taker is because I'm not holding onto any self-judgments or concerns about how I look or if I'm doing it "right." What a great opportunity in that moment to recognize if there are any judgments present with yourself or the person taking the picture. This inner dialogue could sound like this: "I hate having my picture taken. Here I am trying to smile again when it doesn't feel natural. I don't want to be here! Why doesn't Jack just take the #@!% picture already! He's so slow and this feels so unnatural! I hate when he asks this of me! My mouth always looks tense when I'm trying to smile!"

Sound familiar? Do you think there might be just a few judgments present throughout this inner dialogue? Imagine how empowering it would feel in the moment to recognize the judgments and, as an act of self-love, give yourself the voice to express your needs. In this case, it might simply be the act of telling the person that's taking your picture, "If you want me to look natural, you need to evoke the feelings from me that you'd like to see. Be the joy, the trust and the authentic presence. Otherwise, don't ask me to smile." This might cause them to pause and question what you're talking about, but hey, how do we change a paradigm that's not supporting us unless we speak up? This is a simple act of self-honoring and, when we honor our needs, we don't have the tendency to hold onto resentments in the form of judgments.

I Look Good

By Karen Drucker

I have always HATED having my picture taken. It has felt painful and stress-ful, and it gave my inner critic a chance to have her way with me. She would make note of every flaw, wrinkle and reason why I was not one of the "pretty girls" and how I had no right to sparkle and shine in front of a camera.

I had two things going against me from the start in regard to this picture-taking concept. One was that my father had a fashion magazine for people in the wholesale trade of the Los Angeles clothing business. I would be the one to model all the kids' fashions. Was it because I was an adorable kid with Shirley Temple ringlets and dimples? No—I was the publisher's kid and I was cheap. My "pay" was that usually I got to keep the clothes that I modeled and my whole closet was made up of ill-fitting samples from a discontinued clothing line from the year before that I never really liked, but which were free.

The other thing that didn't help is that I grew up in Hollywood, where the idea of what was beautiful was drilled into my head at a very early age. To be deemed acceptable you needed to have long, blonde straight hair (à la Peggy Lipton of the *Mod Squad* TV show); a petite body; year-round sun-kissed tan and a button nose. It also helped if you were named Buffy, Mindy or Britney, and if you could flip your long blonde hair and roll your eyes whenever you said something deep and meaningful like "Oh, my Gawd."

At twelve years old I was fully developed, had acne and braces, straightened my hair and clearly was not one of the "beautiful people" of Hollywood. So when the Hungarian photographer for my dad's magazine, MaRtin, (pronounced with a very exaggerated tongue roll on the R) would shout

out at me modeling a bathing suit in the dead of winter in his thick Hungarian accent: "Come on, Kareeeennnn, pleaazeee, you can do better than that—smile, sparkle, shine!!!!" I would try to smile and look like I was Christie Brinkley—all the while hoping the rubber bands on my braces didn't show or break as I smiled and opened my mouth like he wanted in the shot.

As an adult, I struggled with this poor self-image for years, always dreading any publicity shot I had to take. All those years of humiliation would haunt me like ghosts of photos past. I had the ability to "turn it on," but, truthfully, I was acting and not ever feeling like I had anything worthy to offer or that I was truly beautiful.

Something changed when I turned fifty. For some mysterious reason at this milestone age, something clicked in me. It was as if that inner critic finally decided she was just sick and tired of her job and suddenly, without warning, quit. I found myself having more patience with myself and dumping some of that old baggage that I had been carrying for years. As my friend, author Alan Cohen, says—when you have told your story more than three times you should be done with it. I just felt done with the old "poor-me-I-am-just-not-pretty-enough" sob story.

It also helped to change my thinking when I heard the story of Evy McDonald. Evy was a nurse, living in the Midwest, who was diagnosed with ALS: Lou Gehrig's disease. Given the fact that she was in the health care field, she knew exactly what this disease was going to do to her, and she was determined not to go to her grave hating her body as she always had. She decided to do an experiment and created an exercise where every day she would look at herself in the mirror, and she began making lists of all that she saw about her body. In the beginning the list was quite negative, but after practicing this new form of self-care, day by day the list became more compassionate, self-loving and empowering.

Eventually a miracle occurred where she cured herself of this disease. Evy is now a minister who teaches the power of love and self-acceptance in churches around the country.

I was so inspired and moved by this story that I thought I needed to do this exercise and stand in front of the mirror naked. Oy. The judgments, the shame, the not-good-enoughs. The "If only I could just lose ten pounds, THEN I would be OK" syndrome. I am making it a daily practice to drop that voice of shame and judgment and focus on the good and have love and compassion for myself. I even wrote a chant to help me remember called, "I Will Be Gentle with Myself." The lyrics say, "I will be gentle with myself and I will hold myself like a newborn baby child." When I think of how I would treat a small child I get the feeling inside of how I want to treat myself.

And taking pictures? Well, it's still not my favorite thing to do, and that's OK with me. Each photo session is like some kind of marker for me to see how far I have come. I allow myself to feel *all* the feelings that come up be-forehand—the not good enough, pretty enough, thin enough, etc., etc., and let them just roll over me like clouds passing by. By the time the photographer starts clicking away I can let the true me, the real me, the beautiful me come through. When I am gentle with myself anything is possible.

> *"I finally realized that being grateful to my body was key to giving more love to myself."* —Oprah Winfrey

I Look Good

Song inspired by Evy McDonald
Words: Karen Drucker, music: Karen Drucker & John Hoy

I've got this new little game, it's the latest rage.
It's not limited by race, creed, color or age.
I stand in front of the mirror every day,
look at myself from head to toe and simply say:

"I look good. I look good. I look good.
I am the only me that will ever be. I look good."

The rules of the game are specific and precise,
I can't judge or criticize. I have to be nice.
This is the body that I have, it's divine and a gift.
I don't need to lose weight, color my gray or have a face-lift.

"I look good. I look good. I look good.
I am the only me that will ever be. I look good."

This game isn't limited to what's on the outside.
There's my inner world too that cannot be denied.
'Cause who I really am radiates from within,
so I'll open my heart, quiet my critic and dig in.

They say that beauty's skin deep but I know for a fact,
it's not really how you look, but more how you act.
Was I kind to a stranger? Did I give love today?
I can look in the mirror, look at myself and I can say:

"I am good. I am good. I am good.

I am the only me that will ever be.

I look good. I look good. I look good.

I am the only me that will ever be. I'm good."

From Karen Drucker's "Shine" CD, TayToones Music BMI 2009

living in the tao

The Chinese have an ancient term known as the Tao, which has a variety or blend of meanings. I will simply call it The Way, or The Path. In *Star Wars* terminology, it would be known as The Force. There are countless moments throughout each day to step back and notice whether we are living in this balanced state of the Tao.

One recent example involved exercising on a treadmill aboard a cruise ship amidst rocky waters. My routine consisted of intervals of walking and running. Gradually, I became distinctly aware of my balance, or lack of it. I chose not to hold onto the side rails and while in running mode, there were moments when my shoes would slightly step off the moving platform and make a squeaking sound. Rather than seeing this as a problem, I chose to place my attention on where my attention was being placed! I noticed that when I was thinking too much about needing to stay in balance, there would often be more moments of being out of balance with my feet beginning to sway to the sides. This also would happen when I tried to place a fixed focus on something in front of me.

But, at moments when I allowed my eyes to have a soft focus without targeting anything in particular, I would simply be with the rocking and at one with the treadmill, moving in the same direction with the entire machine. Throughout this time, my balance and my feet would remain centered on the moving platform and there would be an ease and grace-fulness in my movement. This experience served as a simple reminder of when I was feeling at one with my environment, rather than trying to fix, analyze or control the situation.

What experiences in your life serve as examples to remind you whether you are saying "Yes" to the Tao in each moment? What is the path of least resistance right now, your natural way, the balance, the perfect equilibrium? How in this moment can you begin to cultivate a practice of allowance in your life, of feeling into each moment and, without trying, move with the natural rhythm that is calling you?

On the same ship, while eating lunch I overheard a conversation at the table next to me *(not difficult to do since the tables are a foot apart!)*. A man was explaining that he wasn't feeling seasick, just uneasy and that he was finding it challenging to walk with all of the ship's rocking motion. As he looked out at the ocean, he couldn't tell whether he was walking with the ship or against it.

I sat there thinking that being unclear if we're walking in life's natural rhythm or against it was a great metaphor for life. I wanted to turn to him and say, "You can't figure this out with your rational mind; you must *feel* into the rhythm."

As he continued speaking about other issues, his voice had tones of frustra-tion and I actually heard him say that he had to figure this out rationally. I'm not suggesting that rational thinking doesn't have its place in our lives, of course it does. I'm learning that there's mastery in distinguishing when rational thinking serves us and when it's of benefit to feel within and find our balance with life's perfect equilibrium.

Living in the Tao is synonymous with recognizing that every single thing in life is at one with itself. There are no divisions between ourselves, others or events. The idea that we are separate from others and our experiences is an illusion. Using the example of a sports activity is a great, simple illustration of this principle…

I experienced a vivid reminder of being in the Tao through the act of bowling *(yes, I did say bowling!)*. As a bit of the back-story, I learned to bowl when I was ten years old, never becoming a really good bowler, but maintaining a decent average throughout my early adult life. I never practiced consistently enough to hone a reliable skill, so my scores would be all over the place.

In my early twenties, I was out for a fun evening with a group of friends at a local bowling alley. My mind was in a deeply open and perceptive state as I stepped up to the line. Holding the ball in my hand, I became acutely aware of my thoughts as my eyes gazed down the alley at the desired target of pins.

I swung my arm backward, and as it naturally moved forward with momentum, I aimed my thumb toward the pins as I had always done, except that this time I became vividly aware of my thoughts as I released the ball. I noticed that at that split moment of release, if my thoughts were the least bit distracted, I did not hit my desired mark. I became aware that I was either placing my attention fully on being at one with the target, or I was distracted through various thoughts or by outside activities.

Every time that I released the ball from a "non-thinking" modality in which I simply said yes to what I already knew, I hit the exact pins needed to get a great score. Having had years of experience in knowing what it feels like when I got a strike or hit my desired mark, I was able to call on that experience and apply it every time I swung.

The trick or art lies in being in the present moment and honoring what I already know at that precise moment of release. Consequently, I end up having a run of four strikes in a row, noticing that every time I get a strike, it feels exactly the same. There is no thinking involved, no forms of effort or control. It's simply a joy-filled allowance to be in that natural rhythm, fully believing that there are no obstacles in my way.

Perhaps that's what the experience of Oneness is all about, fully knowing without a shadow of a doubt that there are no barriers or obstacles in our way? I've had enough experiences along this line to know that when I am fully feeling at one with each act that I'm taking, everything lines up in the perfect positioning whether it involve a series of bowling pins, my career or my intimate relationship.

Let's apply this principle to having your picture taken. What would it be like to be in front of a camera and fully embody the present moment, now…now…and now? Can you imagine how powerful an experience that would be? Every picture would be a true reflection of your multi-dimensional, magnificent self!

There would not be one false image, meaning that no image would reflect any trace of fear. Every facial muscle would be relaxed. Your eyes would penetrate every frame with a rich and captivating sense of clarity, reflecting your true essence. Spontaneity would emerge and a variety of poses would come naturally. The freedom to play, dance or be pensive would express through you in each passing moment, revealing a rich palette of colors. What a treat it would be to view this glorious bouquet as a way of honoring and remembering the fullness of who you are.

The Present

By Dr. Joe Dispenza

One of my first childhood memories is of being uncomfortable while having my picture taken. I was about three years old and sitting on the marble table in our living room with my brother. John, who was just one year older than I, was beaming and smiling away, click after click, while I sat there suspiciously sensing that this agenda was not for me.

I remember thinking that this was the most ridiculous thing I had experienced in my short life. This total stranger, the photographer, was trying way too hard to make me smile and he just couldn't pull it off. In fact, I noticed that his intention was creating the exact reverse effect within me. I was getting more irritated and self-conscious as time went on. As any pure child, I immediately sensed that something was wrong.

I innately knew that the more he forced himself into my space and tried to make me respond by smiling to such acts of rotund nonsense, the more unable I was to relax, trust the process and be myself. Why? How could I be myself when he wasn't being himself?

The photographer, in his verbosity and over-exaggeration, was not being the least bit authentic with me and I intuitively understood this. Because of his contrived performance, I immediately distrusted him. In spite of my reaction, he carried on anyway and the more he persisted, the more it felt like I was being forced to do something I didn't want to do.

I can still recall the second I felt this new emotion. I became totally frozen in fear with a false sense of "too much self-awareness." As a result, I just wanted the whole thing to be over.

At that young an age, it was difficult for me to put those feelings into words. Today, as an adult, these are the words I would offer that child to say, "How can you capture me in my natural state when I feel so utterly unnatural? The me you are photographing is not me."

Meanwhile, the photographer's actions were not completely in vain. My brother was sitting fully upright with his hands on his knees, putting on a big juicy smile. What contrast; it was "the agony and the ecstasy." Four decades later, those photos still sit on my mother's mantle with my brother John posing so light-hearted and free. And then, there was me, frowning in utter disdain.

Psychology preaches that our first childhood experiences write the script of who we become. To tell the truth, I've noticed pangs of those uneasy feelings in my adult life when I've had to pose for pictures. Not the case when I am lecturing, playing a sport or doing something where my attention is not on myself. During these moments, I am in the flow and there is a natural propensity for me to let go. When I'm not being conscious of myself, I am beyond the boundaries of my inauthentic self, the one fueled by my early childhood trauma.

As the need for having my picture taken increases, I'm constantly made aware of that inauthentic moment from over forty years ago. It's that second where I actually have to freeze, notice how I am being or what I am doing, and then put on a fake smile. Being overly self-aware, just so people can capture one instant in time. To freeze and to pose is contrary to the flow of the true self.

I've been asked countless times by my staff to get new photos taken, always telling them that we didn't need new pictures of me. They insisted in wanting fresh photos and headshots for various purposes such as websites and marketing. Each time they queried, I'd laugh and tell them, "Maybe some other time." But my message to the world is about personal change and overcoming one's self. So in time, I wanted to face this hurdle.

In walks Carl Studna.

When Carl first began taking my pictures, he seemed to be trying pretty hard in getting me to let go and have fun with him, and I began to recall that same familiar feeling from childhood. I became rigid and disassociated. I shook my head and said to myself, "This isn't it for me." It felt too contrived "to try to be natural." I was turned off. And I couldn't follow all of those instructions…"Sit up, now drop your shoulder, lean forward, now drop your chin, now open your eyes wide, now here we go…smile!" All of the instructions were making me feel inauthentic and totally self-conscious. I was three years old again.

But there came a moment when Carl and I began to connect and laugh a bit. In his wisdom and with perfect timing, he set the camera down and we began to get to know each other. I started to let go and began playing with him and he with me. He thus started to coax something out of me. I forgot about "the process" because I forgot about me. I was no longer self-conscious. I see that letting go is about totally losing yourself in the moment as you begin to forget about "you." This is the creative moment.

And that's the sign of a great photographer. Something amazing happens when the artist's vision gets you to the point where you are no longer conscious of yourself, your body or anything other than the "now-present moment." You expand beyond the conscious instant of trying to be a specific materialization of you. This takes place when you get out of your own way.

As I began to let go and release care about whether the pictures came out good or bad, I started having fun and began playing. I tossed the brain about and joked around with Carl. As a result of my willingness to be playful, I believe it allowed Carl to loosen up with me as well. Once we entered into that expanded state, a relaxation began to emerge. I was no longer thinking about being stiff or frozen, but, in fact, I was flowing and no longer caring about anything. We were creating from a state of true spontaneity. I believe that's when the magic started happening and we captured some really great shots.

When we are in the flow and not conscious of ourselves, our attention is not focused on how we look and we're not thinking about results. In these moments of release, we're not concerned about our bodies or what's going on around us. We're simply giving ourselves to the moment. We are present and relaxed; we are the flow and the true self can be captured by the camera.

Being in the flow is a great antithesis to being frozen moment to moment. When our picture is taken, we're at a choice to freeze and put on a mask or allow ourselves to surrender to something greater than the outcome, that being the present moment. This is the shift and opening that took place during our shoot.

We are truly at our best and being our most authentic when we make the shift from trying to force or control an outcome to surrendering to whatever outcome happens, often something far greater than we could have imagined. This choice can be a moment-to-moment practice. When we give ourselves permission to simply relax, let go and trust, the magic really happens.

• • •

Dr. Joe's story demonstrates an act of letting go into the Tao of the moment. When we were in the midst of the session, I recognized that my approach of being silly, talking fast and giving detailed directions was not working for him (*whereas for many people, it's quite effective*).

It's my responsibility as a professional to discern what shooting approach resonates with each subject. I remember thinking at the time that if we continued in the way things were going, the session would need to end really soon and I would not have been successful in getting a wide variety of great shots. Not to mention that Dr. Joe would have walked away feeling drained and frustrated!

Living in the Tao required that I shift my attention from trying to get a result to a deeper listening into what changes and openings needed to occur in that moment. What was being asked to emerge? Authentic, spontaneous play is what called itself forth and everything shifted once he began the game of "Tossing The Brain." It really doesn't matter who thought of the shift. Perhaps we both thought of the idea simultaneously!

I simply know that I am always committed to being as present as I can be in listening and honoring the flow. Out of releasing any attachment to the way that things need to look or how they need to unfold arises the perfect approach that honors everyone's needs in that moment.

Once we made the shift in activity, the entire energy transformed from one of strain to one of play, creativity and ease. Following this shift, I was able to give Dr. Joe directions in as concise a manner as before, but because he was now in the flow and relating to the energy, he was able to follow my cues without feeling tight. There was no longer any resistance present.

This is a great example of being authentic to what the deeper calling is asking of me. My initial intention when we began the shoot was to find an authentic way of playing and having fun with Dr. Joe. Since the first approach was not in resonance with his way of being, it required a deeper listening and letting go to discern what path would lead to his genuine, playful spirit.

Once the breakthrough occurred, it's as if a light entered the room and we had a great time bantering with each other in a playful way. We entered the Tao, that effortless, fluid and creative zone where miracles and mastery abound! The result was a wide variety of alive, connected and powerful images.

remembering self-love

Irecently did a photo session with Barbara, who initially thought that her purpose for doing the shoot was to get some beautiful pictures with her two daughters and grandchildren. As the day approached, I received a call from Barbara telling me that there had been some family drama and the children and grandchildren would not be making it. Barbara trusted the way that everything was unfolding must be for a higher purpose, and she chose to keep her appointment with me.

As Kokeeta, my makeup woman, and I walked up the entryway to Barbara's stunning Spanish-style home, I could not help but notice a most colorful and magical-looking garden on my left. The arched entry door opened to a striking-looking woman in her early sixties with gray, shoulder-length hair and a brilliant, open smile.

Barbara invited us in and, to my surprise, her daughter Jackie was standing in the hallway holding a tiny Chihuahua. As she greeted us with an inviting smile, I thought, "Jackie is in her early thirties…she is as strikingly beautiful as her mother…and plans must have changed."

Jackie had flown in from New York to be with her mother and it was clear that there was uncertainty as to whether Jackie would be in any of the pictures. I quickly discovered that amongst other things, Jackie had done some modeling in New York and was a successful stage actress.

Before arriving, Barbara had mentioned that taking pictures by herself would be a great exercise in self-honoring and in giving to herself in a way that was new for her. Now, she talked in greater detail about how nervous she was to do this session, as she had never done anything like this before and the emphasis of attention had always been on her family. As Kokeeta and I walked with the two women into the kitchen, it was clear that I was entering into a complex family dynamic. Kokeeta began her masterful work of applying makeup to Barbara as I took a look around the house and gardens and came up with some great locations for shooting.

I enthusiastically shared my vision of where we could shoot and how stunning it would be to take some pictures in the garden. I watched Jackie's interest pique as my conversation with Barbara continued. Jackie playfully wrapped her dog's head with a scarf and the very first picture of the day was a close-up of this Chihuahua's face with its wide eyes greeting the camera. She looked like a cross between Yoda and Mother Teresa!

I immediately showed the digital image to Jackie and Barbara and we all shared a lengthy belly laugh at this endearing and comical photo. That image instantly won over Jackie's heart. Before long she was expressing interest in being included in some of the shots along with desiring some solo headshots for her acting career. Of course I was open to this, but made it clear that we would first focus on a variety of Barbara's portraits in various locations. Once we felt complete, we'd move on to the mother-and-daughter portraits and headshots of Jackie.

The first location was the radiantly colorful garden and I had Barbara pose against a wooden statue with cheerful flowers popping out in the background. The pictures were stunning and I took a break to gleefully share some images with Barbara. Before she had a chance to see any pictures in my camera's viewing screen, she quickly moved her head away in what felt like an ancient, conditioned reflex and said, "Oh no, I can't look at these!" My heart reached out to her as I understood her discomfort in viewing her beautiful pictures.

Barbara's response did not come as a surprise to me. In my thirty-plus years of photographing people, I continually witness a large percentage of folks who find it painful viewing pictures of themselves. Their inner critic seems to be easily triggered along with all past conditioning related to self-image that needs to be healed.

I assured Barbara that the pictures looked gorgeous and encouraged her to take a quick glance. Trusting my suggestion, she turned her head to view the image. Following a brief glimpse, she whipped her head away from the screen saying, "No, it's too much!" I honored her need and we resumed taking portraits in a variety of locations.

As a child growing up and in her role as a mother, Barbara had rarely given to herself. It was always about giving to others. She felt deeply uncomfortable having the focus solely on her, as if it were a self-indulgent act. I continually reminded her that it was time to say "Yes" to the magnificent, powerful, wise and beautiful person that she is...on all levels! The day continued to unfold with ease and grace and the most magical pictures emerged.

Barbara was fairly comfortable being in the poses throughout the picture-taking process; it was in the viewing that she felt challenged. Following each location, I encouraged her to view one of my favorite images. Little by little, Barbara was able to spend more moments looking at her pictures and, with utter surprise, she began to really like what she saw! She couldn't believe that these beautiful images were of her.

As we reviewed all the images at the end of the shoot, both Barbara and Jackie commented on what a spiritual and healing experience the day had been. Far beyond the act of picture taking, we all knew that a deeper sense of honor and self-love had emerged throughout the day's activities. We had tangibly experienced the beauty, wisdom and light at the core of these two women, reflected through this most revealing medium.

Years ago, I was hired to take solo portraits of a select group of key executives at a high-functioning New York ad agency. The day was going smoothly with each person arriving on time for their allotted time slot. At 2.00 p.m., Mary walked in the door with her head and shoulders drooping; her fresh, professionally made-up face and hair seemed to wilt as well. The first words out of her mouth were to tell me that her father used to be a professional photographer, and while she was growing up, he had always used her as a model against her will.

As a result of these early torturous years, Mary had grown up hating having her picture taken. Now, the only reason that she was standing before me was because she was ordered to do so. She viewed this process as an intrusion, and a part of her clearly felt violated. I shared my deep respect and assured her that I would be as kind and sensitive as possible.

As the shoot began, it became immediately evident that Mary's facial muscles were so constricted that unless some deep release was to take place, the portraits would be most unflattering and unusable. The usual "bag of tricks" that I brought forth as tools for opening and providing a greater sense of trust were not effective with Mary. It became clear that I must be present with her in the most tender and loving of ways. I must truly see her inner child that felt so violated and speak to her from a compassionate place of love and understanding that truly honored her.

As the session progressed, I witnessed Mary beginning to open. Her eyes began to engage with mine and with the camera lens. The muscles around her mouth began to relax just a little, and her breathing became fuller. I continually reminded her that she was safe and let her know how beautiful she was. I let her know that I honored her for exactly who she was and expressed what a gift she was to the world.

Still photography is a unique craft because it freezes one moment at a time. In the case with Mary, one moment would look tight and terrified while the next brought a reminder of love, thus looking safer and more at peace. I was able to get a few moments that reflected her letting go into a greater sense of feeling loved, just for being herself. In these moments, she knew at her essence that she was perfect and she didn't have to try to look good or be a certain way for the camera. After the shoot, she commented on how deeply she appreciated my way of being with her and that it actually felt like being in a great therapy session!

I could not have received a greater compliment. I felt deeply honored that I had been given the opportunity to share a brief glimpse of time with

Mary in serving as a reminder of the grace, beauty and perfection that is the truth of her nature.

Where in your life do you have subtle or blatant thoughts like Mary's? Perhaps there are insecurities, feelings of being wounded and limiting thoughts that pass through your awareness and cause your breath to become shallow, your neck to tighten or your shoulders to droop? Where is the light of self-love needing to shine in your day-to-day awareness?

Take a moment right now to go within. Allow yourself to fully breathe in these qualities that are asking to be infused into your body and throughout your entire energy system. Let them fill you with their brilliance and their guidance, igniting every cell of your body with their light and their inspired vision. Now, imagine taking these qualities into your next photo session, having them be a source of guiding light. Imagine a beaming light streaming out of a lighthouse and this focused light is filling every part of your being while in front of a camera. Your qualities might be love, joy, freedom, wisdom or success. Allow them to flood their brilliant light through every part of your being while every click of the camera is affirming these truths.

This is a most powerful practice to take into a photo session. It aligns the Universe with your deep intentions. Every time that old, unsupportive thoughts come forward, simply give yourself the devoted time to bring these qualities forward through this visualization practice. If need be, you can ask to take a short break, take some private time and bring forth these light-filled qualities. Remember, having your picture taken is meant to be an honoring process! Let it be a devoted time of saying "Yes" to the full expression and truth of your life...what a unique opportunity.

Photos of My Life

By Dan Kessler

Parts of my life that once had meaning now rest quietly in my own personal photo museum. There are hundreds of evocative vignettes from serious to whimsical, capturing holidays, birthday parties, sports teams, school events, road trips, community affairs, portraits and career achievements; each one telling of a life well-lived, memorized and held safe. My childhood is still reachable—lying in dark slide trays and fading photo envelopes shoved high on my garage and closet shelves. These dusty vaults are carried through life, like stacks of old books, moved around and stored again in the photographer's graveyard.

Throughout childhood, I liked posing for the camera. I was silly, a terror on wheels, a ham! I see myself standing and teasing my sister in her pretty birthday dress, and muse as I pick up another batch of old photos, murmuring, "I loved that stinky pet turtle." And who are all these grownups and kids running around at my birthday parties? What vacation was that? I see faded recollections of Thanksgiving dinner in 1958, my seventh-grade school dance in 1967, me in bangs and a checkered JC Penney flannel shirt at some holiday gathering. At fourteen years old I'm three hundred feet into ascending the cables of Yosemite's Half Dome—then instantly recalling my girlfriend Sharon and me climbing that monument again two years ago with her first harrowing dare to face the steep granite, steadying the panic of a one-thousand-foot drop on each side... I boomerang to being ten and surfing long board in San Diego. Turning another one over, I see there is no date, but guess that I was eight or nine at camp in Big Bear Lake. Next comes a photo that's out of order that fast forwards to age seventeen and I'm skim boarding my old plastic Bon Aire at the Malibu Colony. I view them all with an affectionate yearning.

I cart these boxes from home to home, as I don't want to let go of who I was—wanting to keep my identity close where I can see and touch each picture when it calls to me. Dropping into my photo cemetery feels cozy and comforting, whenever I steal an hour or two, to sit and gaze…to remember. Through black and whites or faded colors, I renew a warm connection to an illusion long gone. On birthdays, some force magnetically pulls me to my childhood at the top of the closet shelf. The soulful routine carries a slight trepidation in opening up that first container of old photos. I know the trip is going to grab hold of my heart and squeeze. I've worked on emotional freedom over the years, and now I open myself to let these images move me down a wide river of sensation. With new acknowledgment I can rub my fingers over the faded Kodak paper and let Niagara Falls cascade down my cheeks, with such sweet return.

Taking out a weathered box and holding these photos is one of my most enjoyable experiences each year. It satiates my desire to reconnect, and usually brings a tactile wonder full of amusement at all the fine fun photos frozen on film (say that ten times fast!). I whisper quietly lots of "Wows," "Ooohs," and "Ahhs," smiling with such *naches*. Of course I've seen the photos countless times. It always brings a long drawn-out wonder as lips proclaim, "Oh my God, look how young Mom and Dad were." I remember that T-Ball uniform, the YMCA swim contest, picnics on Santa Monica Beach. I laugh at how funny the clothes were.

With a pause I dive into a sling-shot recoil in black-and-white, being five years old at a backyard BBQ on Grandma Maybelle's lap. "Whoa," realization strikes me. I'm older now than she was in this photo! Time dysmorphia plays tricks, seeing her young and beautiful. I chuckle at that realization while being somehow drawn into the photo—almost feeling her loving arms on me, smiling and holding me while Grandpa Josh is smoking one of his big cigars and handing me a Roy Rogers cowboy hat. I laugh quietly remembering how Grandpa was always promising he'd get me a horse like Trigger if I was a good boy. I stare at this photo every year to laugh and wipe away the welcome primal tears for my Grandpa and Grandma who I loved so much.

A few months after my fortieth birthday I had a small stroke, leaving me temporarily disabled, forcing me to lose my business and cushy lifestyle in Los Angeles. I moved my family from our lovely five-bedroom home with the custom pool I had built, to a 300 sq. ft. unfinished loft my ex-father-in-law had constructed in a 30' x 90' storage barn on five acres of forest by a lake on the coast of Oregon. I arrived smack in the middle of winter where the rain falls 125 inches a season on a dry year. I recall staring into the camera when someone would take a picture and wanting the lens to catch my bitterness in what I see now as a feeble, angry glare.

Photos show honestly and clearly my state of mind at that time. Looking in hindsight, I can hardly believe these events actually happened to me. One month's pictures show a guy flying high in Southern California sunglasses, Nordstrom shirts and Birkenstocks. Six months later, I'm seen in nearly every photo wearing $3.95 heavy padded long-sleeve flannels, second-hand sweaters, stained jackets and rain gear from the Goodwill store; always holding tightly to my best friend (a walking stick). I can't help but cringe seeing myself so desolate, nearly immobile. I recall how I walked in slow motion and how complicated sentences and thoughts were to form. A part of me wanted to stoically shy away, hide and not have any photos taken throughout this "crash and burn" period of my life.

The true magic of photos is how they show all parts of a man's life. Photos are a symphony of movement and obsession caught forever, played and replayed with such passion, taking over one's senses and sending us back into all the stories of who we were at any given moment.

Throughout time, I never get tired of seeing through pictures everyone in my life together! As more and more memories fade, the pictures hold me to people and circumstances. I know it was real. It happened. I'm reminded that I was there when I can touch the antique glossy and distinguish that I didn't dream it. Desperately I keep photos of myself hoping I'll stay strong and healthy and not get Alzheimer's or a debilitating stroke and forget everything. I want those memories cemented into my neural maze, able to bring the records out and taste every last drop of ecstasy.

And yet on the flip side I ask, "Who really cares about holding onto the past? My life is now and onward. Wind in my sails. Eyes to the horizon!" Photos are things that are done with, never coming back again, and it's surely folly to relive our life sitcom over and over, no matter how cute or handsome, fun or noteworthy we think we are. Would a wise, kindly monk say this is merely Attachment? Would the monk advise, "Pick three favorite photos. Then two. Then one. Then toss them all away. Be free! Start each day unencumbered by your past"? I also ask, "If it feels great and I love it, is that such a bad thing?"? It brings me to Siddhartha's guidance, listening to my heart soar in each transformative moment. My photos are the river of evidence I sit with and listen to as they tell me, "I was here."

We now live in a digital age where film is becoming extinct. Photos fly like the wind across Spaceship Earth, living mysteriously in compressed file boxes, stored pixels within the confines of Internet Servers, instantly recalled with secret passwords. We have immediate spectators for our captions, accompanied with coded messages to social networks, friends and commercial ventures. I love the twenty-first-century photographic arrest where iPhones, Flip Cameras or Droids with nearly unlimited capacity grasp us dancing and reaching skyward, or in front of foaming waves at the shore. I have hundreds of portraits, smiles, zany puckered brows, instant collections of photo frames showing my every nuance, which beg to be released into online albums. Everyone who has a cell phone is a photographer now.

And should my garage burn down? I'd be sad losing the old faded paper of youth. Then I'd let the past go. All my current imagery of fun and excitement is…whoosh…downloaded or uploaded for the entire planet to see. Not a lot of well-used boxes are necessary in this new age. That certainly saves trees! Not a lot of toxic darkroom chemicals being washed down the drain for antiquated methods unless pursued by new or old artists, for art's sake. No worries for film or processing…it's the Wild West with few concerns for cost to click click click and save one's life on camera. The Internet is clean, leaving dusty containers behind for a generation casually using Photoshop tricks that once paid masters for years of experience.

Such is my life and evolution of the photo.

what are you hiding?

The first thought that comes to mind when considering this question is the well-known passage from Marianne Williamson entitled, "Our Deepest Fear."

Our deepest fear is not that we are inadequate.
Our deepest fear is that we are powerful beyond measure.
It is our light, not our darkness, that most frightens us.
We ask ourselves, Who am I to be brilliant,
gorgeous, handsome, talented and fabulous?
Actually, who are you not to be?
You are a child of God.
Your playing small does not serve the world.
There is nothing enlightened about shrinking
so that other people won't feel insecure around you.
We are all meant to shine, as children do.
We were born to make manifest the glory of God within us.
It is not just in some; it is in everyone.
And, as we let our own light shine, we consciously give
other people permission to do the same.
As we are liberated from our fear,
our presence automatically liberates others.

One of the most common themes that people discuss when having their picture taken is that they feel vulnerable in front of a camera and that the camera somehow exposes them in a way that feels uncomfortable. I often sense that there's an unspoken inner dialogue that's thinking, "Others will see something about me that I'm afraid to let them see." Usually, the concerns have to do with criticism over physical appearance, but what if that's not really the deal? Perhaps underneath the physical façade is the discomfort in truly shining our light, our brilliant and unique essence? I deeply relate to Marianne's quote and the truth that I witness in my own life related to letting my light shine. Whether I'm in a session with someone or out in the world, I am constantly reminded that when I am fully expressive, it gives others the unspoken permission to follow suit and release their inhibitions.

The Feather

By Raymond Aaron

I was on a driving vacation once and found myself near an Indian reservation that boasted a special waterfall. So I stopped to enjoy the view and indeed found it to be very beautiful. Though the waterfall was grand and a huge tourist attraction, that day the huge parking lot was empty. I parked and walked to the edge of the concrete to view the falls. I was enthralled with its raw beauty and its massive power.

As I watched and enjoyed, another car drove up to where I was standing. An older couple got out and approached the railing near me. They were the most absurd caricature of tourists I had ever seen. They were overweight, sunburned seniors, wearing oversized Bermuda shorts and glaring, gaudy shirts. But worst of all was the fake Indian headband the woman was wearing with a feather sticking straight up from behind her head. She had obviously bought it from the Indian reservation store and was very proud of it. I tried not to stare, but was quite taken by how silly this feather was.

Then the woman asked her husband to take a photo of her with the waterfall in the background. That is a normal tourist request. Heck, we've all done it.

She turned and leaned against the railing with the waterfall behind her. Dutifully, the husband brought out his little point-and-shoot camera and walked a few feet away to take the photo. She instructed him first to walk farther back. Then, to my surprise, she asked him to walk even farther back. At that distance of about thirty feet, I knew that the woman would be a tiny dot in the photo, the background waterfall would also be a tiny dot and the majority of the photo would be the mammoth parking lot in the foreground and the sky in the background. Nevertheless, the woman insisted that her husband back up right to the other end of the entire parking lot, about two hundred feet away. From that distance, the waterfall and the wife would be indistinguishable dots in a photo of a huge parking lot. He took the picture and walked and walked and walked back to his wife.

Luckily I was close enough to hear what she had asked. It has remained in my mind as possibly the most absurd photography question of all time. It took all of my restraint to not burst out in laughter. When her husband was close enough, she asked: *"Did you get the feather?"*

· · ·

How often are you hoping or expecting to "get the feather" when your aim is a million miles off? How accurate is your perception of how big or small you are showing up in your life? How often does your conscious mind think, "I want to be seen and recognized" when your perception of yourself is but a dot on the horizon? How often are you wanting to control someone *(or something)* and directing with such precise certainty and then are pissed off at that person *(or outcome)* because it's not right?

Every moment presents the ripe opportunity to rest in the rich, full body of our authentic nature. When we place our attention on simply sinking into that peaceful place within, we have no need or desire to compare ourselves to anyone else. From this still place, it's simply natural to fully give of ourselves with each passing moment. The truth is that we are most radiant at our core, so how can we not shine when the cloak of fear, judgment or separation is no longer present?

reclaiming self-expression and freedom

A young couple and their toddler daughter were sitting in seats on a plane in front of me for a brief one-hour flight. Before and during takeoff, their daughter began to cry, quickly escalating into full-out hysterics. Screaming at the top of her lungs, the child was clearly experiencing deep pain, likely from the change in cabin pressure.

In my perception, the parents were more concerned about quieting the child than nurturing her and discovering the root of her anguish. They were shushing and moving her around as she continued to scream, trying to keep her preoccupied from feeling her pain rather than teaching her how to open her mouth and equalize her ears. I felt a deep sense of compassion for this little girl and wished that I could hold and comfort her with my healing energy.

As the plane rose and reached a consistent altitude with a pressurized cabin, the young girl's pain subsided and her crying ended. I overheard her mother say to her, "Can you tell everyone that you're sorry?" I had to hold back from moving my head into their row from behind and saying, "She has absolutely nothing to feel sorry about. She was clearly experiencing tremendous pain in her ears and it's up to you as her parents to comfort her and determine if there's anything you can offer her that will ease the discomfort." Later in the flight, the father supplied a toy and food that did help to bring their daughter greater comfort.

That brief encounter served as a reminder of how many times as children we can be criticized, scrutinized or embarrassed for simply being honest in expressing our needs. It's clear that these young parents were doing the best they knew how at that moment of crisis. Although they truly wanted to be loving with their daughter, they ended up reacting out of past conditioning and planted a seed in their young daughter's consciousness that she needs to be sorry when she's in pain or when authentically expressing her needs. In that moment, the parents were more concerned about the passengers around them than their daughter's needs. This incident served as a poignant example of the choice we have in each moment to either honor the deeper need that is being expressed or allow fear to dictate our responses.

Several years ago, I had the opportunity to attend a two-day improvisation class led by the Academy Award–winning actor Alan Arkin. The class consisted of about twenty people ranging in age from early twenties to late sixties. Many of these people I already knew as we were a part of the same church community just outside of Denver.

You've probably heard the statistic that most people's biggest fear is public speaking, right? Well, not the case with me. My biggest fear was being in an improv class. I had lived most of my life in Los Angeles, and I would have never taken this type of class while living there because *(in my perception)* the town was filled with actors and they take it all quite seriously. There's no way that I would have put myself in a situation where I couldn't plan anything ahead of time and then be judged by others. That would have been my biggest fear!

In this case, I was in a room with people not involved in showbiz, and most of them, like myself, had never done this before. The other reason I was willing to make this leap was because I held such a strong admiration and respect for our instructor, Alan. I knew that if I didn't choose to attend due to my old fears, I'd really regret the opportunity to work with this master at his craft.

One of the very first things that Alan wanted us to know was that he wasn't interested in seeing us "perform" or use contrived formulas akin to a *Saturday Night Live* skit. He made it very clear that we were not there to please him or to get his approval. He couldn't care less! He simply wanted us to be real, to be fully authentic in whatever spontaneously came through in order to provide richness to each character and a natural flow with those we were teaming with. Hearing this eased my mind because I was reminded that I never have to figure anything out when I'm surrendered to simply being real in each moment. Consequently, the entire weekend was one of the most creative, playful and expressive group experiences I've had as an adult. It served as such a beautiful opportunity to release all judgments toward myself and toward others. We played like little children, simply allowing whatever creative urge that beckoned to have its way. We laughed, we cried, we felt a natural enthusiasm while acting in our skits and while watching others.

This class served as such a strong reminder that when I release "the critic" inside and allow myself to just be in the moment, trusting that the perfect impulse will lead me, it always does. I'm not suggesting that we forego preparing for things in our lives. Professional athletes require years of practice to hone their skills, but once they've built a strong foundation on which to stand, all the great winners will tell you that they were simply in a zone of letting go—a place of allowing their best to flow through in what feels like a divine orchestration.

Are there any areas in your life where you feel held back or restricted in your self-expression? If so, would you say that part of the reason is due to the concern of what others will think? Remember my story about never considering doing an improv class in Hollywood? It took me fifty years to feel safe enough to step out in this way! Was my concern legitimate or mostly a fabricated story fueled by the fear of being ridiculed? Looking back on it, I sense that most of it was made up, and it took the appearance of being far away from Hollywood and in a safe environment for me to take that scary leap.

Take a moment right now and consider the following questions:

- What will it take for me to feel safe enough to fully express my authentic voice?

- Who needs to approve or what condition needs to feel just right in order to be daring?

- What are those things in life that I've been putting off that would be on my "bucket list"?

- If I truly felt that I could not fail and there was nobody judging, how would I be operating in the world and what different choices would I be making?

Now, allow yourself to be honest and answer each question as your innate wisdom surfaces. Make a commitment to sit with each question every day for the next week and see what additional answers surface.

Imagine taking a small step today toward a freer way of expressing your authentic self. It might be singing full-out while in the car driving, or having a more in-depth conversation with the person that serves your morning coffee at Starbucks. I encourage you to start a Self-Expression list and each day agree to express at least one thing on that list. Eventually, your list can become bolder and include classes you've longed to take and hobbies, sports and skills you've been meaning to learn. I'm convinced that if you begin this practice and allow it to grow, you will gradually become fearless in your way of living as you trust that natural, creative impulse that is constantly filling you with inspired vision and inexhaustible forms of expression.

My friend and noted novelist Tom Robbins serves as a brilliant example of someone who chooses to have a creative and playful experience each time that he does a photo session *(at least with me!)*. During my first shoot with Tom, close to thirty years ago, I was so taken by how inventive and light-hearted he was in front of the camera. We were shooting at his vividly creative and eclectic home, and within moments, he brought out a rubber alligator snout and asked if I'd like to take a few shots, face adorned in this mask.

Instantly, we were coming up with all sorts of obscure poses: "Alligator Tommy reclining on a chaise longue reading *Connoisseur Magazine*." "Robbins the reptile, standing stoically in an entryway, holding a carved walking stick." "The mean, green Tommy machine on all fours looking quite formidable."

Throughout the years, I've continued to photograph Tom for his book jackets and for publicity purposes. Each session *(which is more like two kids having a good time)* always brings delightful results because we choose to be present, playful and expressive. I recently asked Tom if he has always felt at ease in front of a camera, and the following is his reply.

Canon Fodder

By Tom Robbins

My one and only modeling assignment was for a glossy magazine called *Sportswear International*. I'm told it is no longer being published, although I'm reasonably sure I can't be blamed (at least not entirely) for its demise.

At the time, I was not particularly well known, so one can assume I was chosen less for any literary celebrity than for my appearance. That—and my friendship with a certain fashion model named Laren Stover, who was also in the shoot.

The shoot took place in a weedy vacant lot on the northern edge of Greenwich Village. I was outfitted in heavily zippered clothing supplied by the hip company Kamikaze; well-named it turned out, since it, too, has since crashed and burned. I liked the clothes, I liked Laren Stover, I was at home in the weeds. The photographer, however....

Throughout the shoot, he kept yelling at me, "Stop smiling!" Over and over, in a thickish, Eastern European accent, "Don't smile! Look sophisticated!"

Well, if nothing else, I learned from that experience why most of the models in fancy fashion magazines appear as if they're painfully constipated. They've been conditioned by photographers, who themselves were conditioned by editors, to believe a joyful countenance is for losers, hicks, and dorks. So, as we leaf through the pages of *Vogue* or *Harper's Bazaar*, let's remind ourselves that while those elegantly attired posers may look neurotic, sour, angst-ridden, and tense, they are in fact simply cooler than you or I. Their homes aren't in foreclosure, they're not secretly under siege from hemorrhoids, nor have their grandmothers recently been eaten by starving baby donkeys. They just happen to be sophisticated.

Incidentally, in subsequent (*decidedly non-fashion*) photo sessions over the years, neither Cade Martin nor Gus Van Sant, neither Carl Studna nor Annie Leibovitz ever attempted to refine my facial expression, a courtesy for which I grin in uncouth appreciation.

Now, for a writer of unconventional fiction, living by choice far from the centers of social and financial ambition, I suppose I've spent more than my share of moments before the camera. If I've enjoyed being photographed whereas many people had just as soon visit the dentist, it has little if anything to do with vanity. Rather, I'm philosophically disposed, for better or worse, to try to incorporate humor and imagination in virtually everything I do—including going to the dentist. There's another reason. Carlos Castaneda, the otherworldly anthropologist, once said that people who look the same in all of their photographs are not real people. Thus warned, I'm always eager to check on the state of my personal reality.

· · ·

Throughout the years, I've always looked forward to photo sessions with Tom because our time together doesn't feel like *I'm* orchestrating a photo shoot with Tom Robbins. Our time becomes a co-creative experience of playing and exploring how this moment and the next can be inventive and downright adventurous!

Maybe Tom's got it right; perhaps it really is that easy to simply decide that experiences in our life can be met with joy and playfulness, choosing not to get too serious or heavy. Imagine being in front of a camera and

simply deciding ahead of time that you're going to make this a fun and light photo session. Wouldn't you trust that every moment of the shoot would be an invitation to be creative, free and fully expressive? Living from that intention, there would not be room for self-judgment or fear-based thoughts. From this purview, you become the initiator of the invitation to be expressive and creative, rather than waiting for others to set the tone. If this is a session devoted to bringing out the fullness of your unique expression and message, you certainly have the permission to make clear with the photographer the approach that works best for you, what supports you feeling relaxed, trusting and free to be fully creative.

Every time that you're in front of a camera you have the opportunity to choose how expressive you'll be in that moment. What quality or aspect of yourself do you feel called to show to the world in that essential moment? Imagine that every time the camera's lens opens and closes with the resonant sound of the click it is asking you, "What do you want to say right now? What do you want others to know about you? What aspect of yourself do you wish to express in *this* moment?"

wild goose chase

Most of us are familiar with the expression, "wild goose chase." How many times have you been running around trying to be, do or act in such a way that is not in accordance with your authentic nature? So many in our Western culture are looking for the "quick fix," the easy remedy that will solve whatever challenge is before us. Whether it's a solution offering weight loss, abundant finances, finding our soul mate, a way to look and feel younger or discover our true innate gifts, millions of people are looking for ourselves in places where we will easily bring forth a feeling of being loved, a sense of security, happiness and a quality of fulfillment. We've become focused on looking for ourselves in places where we will never be found.

I recently had a potent experience that mirrors this condition. On a Friday morning I was about to devote the day to video recording a series of five-minute talks for my wife Cynthia's support network. Everything was technically in place and ready to begin. Pamela, the makeup artist, had just completed her masterful work with Cynthia. I ran to the refrigerator to get a mild pick-me-up before shooting, a glass of iced green tea. I was just about to pour the drink when Pamela entered the kitchen and said, "Would you like to try one of these instead of your drink?" and pulled out a pill with a name that resounded of bold energy. That should have been my first clue.

From adulthood forward, I've always been a person who's pretty attuned to what I put into my body, so I asked what was in the pill. I was assured that it contained only natural ingredients and it was an herbal supplement that was good for the body. I reviewed the ingredients and everything appeared to be natural with no powerful stimulants. There were no traces of caffeine *(as my body reacts in an unpleasant "crash and burn" way with most forms of caffeine, aside from that in green tea)*. With Pamela's strong endorsement ringing in my ears, I decide to give it a try. She advised me that I would not likely feel any effects for about an hour.

I began the videotaping and gradually noticed my body feeling lighter. Intermittently, Pamela would ask, "Do you feel anything yet?"

That should have been my second clue. That question was reminiscent of my teenage years, resurfacing vivid memories of coming on to a variety of drug-induced experiences.

Within an hour, I was feeling REALLY GOOD! I didn't have the agitated, frenetic energy that a cup of coffee would have given me. I simply felt elevated. As I stood or sat in a focused position, the time simply flew by and I was able to shoot each of the thirteen video spots within four hours with virtually no body tension. I was laughing and having a great time between takes and affirming what a great product it was and how I must get some.

That was the "honeymoon stage." Several hours later I was still in a seriously busy mode, wanting to do anything that would keep me active. Before I knew it, it was 8:00 p.m. and I hadn't thought one bit about eating any dinner. That was very unusual for me as I always have a hearty appetite unless I'm really under the weather.

I then recalled Pamela mentioning that the pill could serve as an appetite suppressant. Of course I didn't think that would apply for me. I literally had to force myself to eat some soup and let me tell you, it didn't taste at all good! One of life's daily pleasures that I so value is my appreciation for the subtle tastes found in a vast variety of foods. My world would feel so much bleaker without my daily anticipation of eating, induced by a healthy appetite, not to mention the actual tantalization of the taste buds through my daily ingesting of magnificent morsels!

Fortunately, when Cynthia arrived home at 10:00 p.m., she was feeling naturally hyper from an inspiring meeting, so she wasn't ready for bed until 1:00 a.m. Here I was lying in bed with my eyes staring at the ceiling at 1:30 a.m. I had taken the pill at 10:30 the previous morning and my mind would not stop spinning. I was on a roller coaster that wasn't nearly ready to end. I rarely have any problem sleeping, but on this night there were only brief moments where I experienced a solid state of sleep.

As the sun rose, I could still feel a slight buzz of energy from the substance. However, most of it had left my system and I was able to reflect on the past twenty-four hours. I actually felt a sense of gratitude as many insights flooded forward. I realized that as much as the pill provided a vast reservoir of energy, there was no time during this experience that I felt the least bit connected to Source or my center. I was quite clear that I would not have been the least bit successful if I had attempted to meditate or locate that still place within for peace and guidance. My mind and body had been spinning so quickly I would not have been able to find a place of stillness.

As a child I loved going to amusement parks. My favorite ride involved entering this circular room and being told to stand with my body against the wall. Within moments, the room would begin spinning so quickly that the centrifugal force would cause my body to stick to the wall as the floor dropped beneath me. I thought this was the most thrilling and magical thing that could exist! What a great combination, something that was both thrilling and had a sense of wonder about it.

Perhaps not much has changed as we've grown into adulthood, as we continue to seek that thrilling sensation that reminds us that we're alive. As a child, I certainly had zero interest in being still, nor did I have a clue that we all have a center of wisdom and guidance within us. That was something rarely taught through parents in the fifties and early sixties. Fortunately, I was introduced to a form of meditation at age seventeen that resonated with my soul. Once I experienced a taste of stillness, I knew what I was missing if, through time, I neglected to pay it a visit.

My twenty-four hour "pill" episode gave me a first-hand experience of what it felt like to be completely revved up in the act of doing, with zero emphasis on being guided by or connected to my center or Source. While the experience was taking place, I had felt a great level of accomplishment but little sense of fulfillment. When I'm simply doing without being guided, my ego, or my identity, is running the show. I often think about how many people in this country are motivated by some sort of external stimulant, such as coffee, the idea of success, sex, pornography, looking thin, looking young, having the right car, having the trophy wife or power husband.

By reading more literature about the "nutritional pill," I came to realize that its biggest selling point is helping with weight loss. So, imagine having a legal, over-the-counter substance that you can take daily as a mood enhancer and appetite suppressant while giving you unbridled energy. You'll be thin, happy and successful! Amazing.

Until, that is, you realize that without being guided by your inner compass, none of these activities or symbols will truly feed you at your core. It's like having a diet of all desserts with no true nutrients to uplift and sustain you. The numbers are staggering on how many people *(primarily women)* in the United States are taking some sort of daily "supplement" to assist with weight loss, not to mention the millions of people taking some sort of mood enhancer.

A friend of mine recently shared a story that I found most touching and unsettling. Elaine is in her early fifties and lives in an affluent Southern California community. She was recently having lunch at a restaurant with a few of her women friends. In the course of the meal, Elaine was looking around the table and noticed that every woman present, aside from herself, had experienced some form of cosmetic facial surgery. This fact is not what disturbed me the most.

Her next thought was, "I wonder if any of my friends are looking at me with judgment because I have not chosen to have any work done?" She was actually feeling uncomfortable, questioning if she "fit in" because of her choice to naturally age.

After hearing this story I asked myself, "Is our culture, in its incessant need to look young, developing a new standard of what's acceptable on how we physically age?" Of course, youth is associated with vitality, but isn't youth also a sign of the lack of wisdom and experience that we so preciously gain as we age? Being in my mid-fifties, there are times that I find myself looking in the mirror and thinking, "Man, you are starting to look old!" I have to catch myself and question what's motivating that thought, because underneath the thought is a subtle concern that as I age and look older, society will not take me as seriously, not value my gifts as strongly, and eventually will choose to discard me altogether! And I'm speaking from the male perspective.

Amplify this concern one hundredfold for women because women are judged by their youthful appearance so much more than men. A woman's beauty in our culture is largely based on her youthful physical appearance. It's rare that we see a woman in her sixties through nineties and label her as being beautiful. If we look to certain indigenous cultures, age is something that reflects an individual's wisdom. The aging through life's series of lessons and insights is something to be honored. The lines in one's face represent a richness of the soul's journey and its beauty, bringing a deep sense of value and respect.

Don't you think that it's time that we take a stand and not buy into all of the outside influences *(advertising, commercials, magazines, discussions at the water cooler)* that tell us we need to look a certain way in order to be successful, in order to fit in, in order to be loved? All of these subtle and

not-so-subtle messages are based in the belief that we need to be and look like someone that we're not. Here's a liberating concept:

Our beauty, success and sense of wholeness have NOTHING to do with what others think of us. All that matters is how connected we are to the divine perfection that resides at the core of our being. People naturally admire and respect us when we are anchored securely in who we really are, and in that strength of unique character that is unlike anyone else, we boldly live beyond the old doubts and concerns. It's truly an inside job.

The trick is in not trying to achieve this trait in order to please others. We must choose this path of devotion solely for the purpose of knowing ourselves more intimately, and ultimately to feel at one with our divine creator.

As we stand before the camera's lens, we have the opportunity to claim our magnificent beauty. As nature continues to paint its rich and unique brush strokes through each facial line, through the radiant presence emitting through our eyes, and through the innate wisdom that brilliantly emanates, we can rest in the comfort and stillness of who we truly are, knowing that we are unique and glorious reflections of the Divine.

Ageless Beauty

By Marian Head

At twelve, I went through an awkward stage. Adorned with pre-teen acne, pre-tweezed eyebrows and pre-shaven legs, I was a sight to behold. With the addition of shiny silver braces, my father began saying, "To me, you are beautiful." I knew what that meant.

No wonder I shied away from cameras.

Much later, I used modern photo technologies to brush away my imperfections, which seemed to appear exponentially as I aged. At age fifty-seven, I heard a woman lament, "I feel *guilty* about what I look like as I get older." I felt—and shared—her pain.

As I hiked along the Oregon Coast that summer, her oft-remembered words filled my mind. Yet in Nature's majesty, they rang hollow. For all around me I saw the magnificent results of aging. Rocks and caves proudly showed their purple scarring and other "imperfections" from their relationship with life. Ancient, gnarled trees commanded my respect and elicited my admiration for their persistence and tenacity over decades of battering winds and rain. Millennia of intimacy between cliffs and surf produced jagged deviations along the ever-maturing coastline. Nature's Spirit gently guided me to notice the exquisite beauty in aging. In a moment of illumination, I realized that I too am NATURE. I have always loved basking in the sun, playing in the water, dancing with the wind.

Like the trees, the rocks, the calcified cliffs...wouldn't I expect to be carved and colored and distinguished by my lifetime of interaction with

Mother Nature? Indeed, wouldn't it be a privilege to wear the signs of my cherished relationship with the elements of which I am One?

Perhaps. Yet at nearly sixty, my body is still fit, the signs of aging surely not as visible to others as to myself. How will I feel when I am obviously and irreversibly weathered?

When the mirror reflects back to me the changes sculpted by life's precious experiences, I trust my newfound spiritual perspective will hold steady. As the self-consciousness of my youth continues to give way to greater Consciousness of Self, I will welcome the camera as a way to capture and radiate the truth of Who I Am (*and You Are*): Nature's magnificent models of aging beauty.

every picture tells a story

There is no picture that ever tells the same story, whether it be a person, landscape or still-life. Every year, I offer a photography workshop called, "Embracing the Sacred." I never tire of teaching this class because I'm continually inspired by life's unique displays. As an example, I am constantly in awe of the ever-changing cloud formations billowing over the vast Colorado plains and mountain regions. I'll be driving along and struck by a design that is so complex in its layers, shades and hues. I'll think, "What an amazing and rich tapestry...I've never seen anything like it!"

During the first day, I join the participants in walking the grounds of our class location. With camera in tow, all are asked to open

This way of seeing, of slowing down and honoring the sacred in life's seemingly ordinary moments, is the fundamental message woven throughout the two days of my workshop.

their field of perception to see everything around them in a new and expanded way. This might include exploring new angles, the complex textures of the most seemingly ordinary objects, or the unique perspective seen when you're really close to an object through the "macro world." Suddenly, a blade of grass transforms into its own mammoth-like tree amidst the blurred focus of its surrounding forest of giant blades. It becomes an enchanting universe of its own, rather than just another green lawn.

At day's end, I ask each person to choose their favorite image, have it printed into an 8x10 and bring it to the following class. As each classmate arrives a week later with their picture in hand, there's such a delightful sense of mystery in the air. Everyone places their picture on the floor in a large circle facing outward, and in silence all of us walk in a circle viewing each image. The one reoccurring theme that I notice while viewing this collection of photographs is that no two are ever the same! You might have three people that have taken a picture of the same fountain, yet each picture looks significantly different from the next. One might be closer, the second might show more of the sky, and the third will focus on the droplets of water moving through the air appearing blurred rather than frozen.

There are a number of reasons why this diversity is always present. First and foremost, we live in a Universe that simply is change. Nothing ever remains the same. From the larger cosmic perspective, down to the minutest sub-particle, everything is always moving in this most unique and seemingly random dance. When we remember, or catch glimpses of this truth, not only is our field of perception enhanced, but as every moment tells a new and intriguing story, our sense of wonder and adventure becomes heightened.

Because we're all so complexly different from one another in our life and soul experience, each of us sees and perceives things around us with a vastly different perspective. This truth is often the most evident in our closest relationships. How many times have you been in an argument with your spouse, your mother, your child, your friend or your boss over a different way of seeing things? You and your thirteen-year-old son might agree that his bedroom needs to be kept clean and tidy on a constant basis, yet his version of "constant" is different than yours. You and your wife might both share a flair for how you dress and present yourselves in the world, yet she cannot understand how you'd wear a horizontal patterned tie with a pin-striped suit.

There are so many subtleties in the choices we make from moment to moment and, on some levels, it's quite amazing that we manage to successfully get along with anyone for any length of time! The greater that we're aware and able to consciously honor the uniqueness that lies within each of us, the easier it becomes to live in a place of constant inquiry rather than judgment. "Oh, that's interesting that you find it appealing to mix vertical and horizontal patterns with your clothing. I'm truly curious how, in your eyes, these two patterns mix well together?"

In Buddhism, this way of seeing is known as the Beginner's Mind; living every moment from an open, inquisitive place of genuine inquiry. In our western culture, it can be so challenging to imagine living life in this deep place of non-attachment. This does not mean that we walk around being drones without any of our own distinct opinions; it simply means we're not attached to our opinions or our perceptions. The more that we keep the doorway open to new or expanded ways of seeing, the richer our lives become. We recognize that nothing is stagnant, in fact everything is alive with adventure. Each moment offers the opportunity to feel and express richer dimensions of our being. When we remain open to each other's differences, we're given a key to the richness of diversity that lives at the core of our DNA. We honor how no two people have the same makeup!

Have you ever looked at a picture of yourself and thought, "I love the way that this makes me feel!" There's just something about the moment that's portrayed in the photograph that evokes a certain feeling that makes you feel good. It might be a spontaneous moment where you're looking at someone and you're filled with joy, or a contemplative moment that conveys a deep sense of peace and well-being. It might even be a composite image that lives within your mind and has never manifested into a three-dimensional photograph.

One potent personal snapshot memory is a millisecond frozen in time when I was eight years old. Riding on the Matterhorn roller coaster at Disneyland my face was radiating light, joy and utter wonderment! This composite memory, in the form of a photograph, represents the true adventurous nature at the core of my being, fully embracing the mystery and the exhilaration of life's magical journey! Take a moment for yourself and imagine what that image would look like for you. Do you have a real photograph that reflects one of these blissful moments?

When you reflect back on your life, what memory or image comes to mind that evokes a feeling of pure goodness?

If you have an actual photo that you can access, dig it up and place it on an altar in your home, your desk, or anywhere that you would definitely see it every day.

If you don't have a photograph, write as descriptively as possible about the image or moment, as if it's a real photograph.

- Where are you?

- What are you doing?

- How are you feeling?

- Describe the moment as vividly as possible and name all of the qualities that you're embodying and expressing.

- Once you're complete, place that sheet of paper in the same place you would have placed the actual photograph.

This image, whether in photographic or written form, will serve as a reminder of who you really are at the core of your true nature. I encourage you to take a few moments out of every day to spend with this image. Allow yourself to devote a slice of time to honor this lightness of being, the truth of who you are beyond any daily concerns, any doubts or the illusion of life's hardships.

Several years ago, I was in a most exceptional Master of Arts Degree in Spiritual Psychology program at the University of Santa Monica. During the second year of the program, we were given a very powerful exercise. In this three-month Relationship Project assignment we were to choose the one person that we held the most charge with, the most judgment around unresolved issues. We had to design a weekly practice centered around this person that would ultimately bring forgiveness and a release of our held-in anger, resentment and judgment.

One of my weekly practices involved placing a picture of this person on my altar. By seeing the incredible beauty and innocence at the core of his being, I reached a place of authentically loving this person beyond the circumstances, and a light of forgiveness shone on the situation.

By the end of the three-month period after devotedly practicing this ritual along with several others that I had designed, there was absolutely no charge left with this individual, no judgments, no hurt or anger. I simply felt a deep sense of compassion and love for him and for his life path. Granted, I was not condoning his past actions and behavior; I simply didn't have any need to hold onto the energy behind our shared story any longer. I was free and I felt only a deep love for this person.

I'm sharing this example as a testimony to the fact that this exercise really works. If it's effective when focused on another individual, it will certainly carry the same power and potency when directed at yourself.

Using a photograph in this fashion is a reminder of how powerful a still image can be. Think about it: we have the ability to select precise slices of life, frozen in a fraction of a second. These moments will always be completely honest, showing where our focus and attention is in that exact click of the camera. The candid glimpses often provide a raw reflection of where our attention is being placed when we're not aware of a camera.

I remember in college viewing a candid profile of myself in focused conversation taken at a reception for a group photography exhibition. The first thing that jumped out at me was how poor my posture looked. My shoulders were bent over and I didn't appear to be very confident.

At that first glance, I wanted to burn the picture and send its ashes into orbit! Instead, I chose to take a good study of the image and allow that frozen moment to provide a gem of insight. What did the slumped posture represent in terms of how I presented myself in the world? I began to realize that I had been holding onto an unconscious irrational belief that I shouldn't stand out too much as that was a sign of arrogance.

This reflection served as a rude awakening and I began to place my attention on being more upright in my body and in my way of greeting the world. Rather than resisting the impulse to tear up the picture, I chose to use the insight as a vivid reminder in greeting the world with full gusto and courage, reflected through an aligned back and upright shoulders.

How often do you choose to rip up or delete an image because it's not "flattering," or because it triggers a self-judgment? Just as we have the opportunity to use joyous and freedom-reflecting pictures as a symbol of our perfect nature, so in turn, we have the ability to gain great value and insight from those images that tweak us or provoke a reaction. Wouldn't it be liberating to simply observe what thoughts and feelings arise when viewing photos of yourself, rather than feeling the need to react and instantly form a negative opinion or judgment?

Imagine that you have just completed a portrait session and you're viewing a series of pictures of yourself. How quickly do you have a conditioned response to judge or criticize every image before you? Do you have an immediate reaction telling you that you hate this one because your nose looks too big, or your mouth looks too wide, or your hair isn't right, or you simply think that you look too old? How quickly do you jump to forming a distinct opinion that's laced with a mega-ton of reactive energy?

Believe me, you're not alone! This is a fairly common response with a large percentage of people. One scenario might go something like this: "I can't believe how big my nose looks from that angle. I should never let anyone take profile pictures of me from my left side!" Then, you catch yourself and ask, "Where is this reaction coming from? Is my perception about this really true? My father used to tell me that my nose looked larger when viewed from my left side. Do I really look less flattering or is my perception being influenced by an old event that isn't based in reality? Does this thought and its consequent reaction serve me?"

If you take the time to question and reevaluate these triggered responses as they arise, you will be provided with a rich display of insights that offer a vast array of choices on how to respond while also learning more about yourself and your ability to choose love over condemnation. Just like Karen Drucker's example of standing in front of a mirror and allowing the old judgments to release as she opened to seeing the love, beauty and compassion within, we have that potent ability to observe our thoughts and choose how we perceive and respond in any given moment.

- What if you were able to stop yourself fairly quickly before the litany of self-judgment became all-consuming and ask yourself a few questions?

- What is there for me to learn about myself in this picture?

- What aspects of myself are being reflected here?

- Where am I holding any tension and how can I place my attention on letting it go?

- Which of these images reflect my true essence in its most authentic expression?

- Who is the "I" that I am looking at?

- What judgments am I holding onto that do not support my fullest of expression?

- Who says I don't photograph well?

Viewing portraits can serve as a wonderful opportunity to observe where you store tension in your face. One frame might look completely relaxed and the next could reveal massive tension around your facial muscles. What concerns or fear-based thoughts were streaming into your mind when that shot was taken?

If you are willing to slow down each time you're viewing pictures of yourself and ask these revealing questions, this process will serve as a most insightful reflection and healing of any old patterns or beliefs that have been hindering your complete freedom and self-expression. What a marvelous tool for self-reflection and for realigning with the true brilliance of your authentic nature. The more you're able to track your beliefs and view their corresponding physical reflection in each image, the closer you'll be to mastering a conscious moment-to-moment lifestyle where you choose thoughts that promote freedom, love and full self-expression.

Embracing the Pieces, One Picture at a Time

By Zemirah Jazwierska

On the day of my photo session I arrived with the intention to link a face to the next creative chapter in my life. For years I had told myself that when I was ready to take my creative career to the next level and become more publicly visible, I would invest in a professional photo shoot. That time had come. I felt some percolating inner uncertainties, but I was determined to leap into the Divine net and open once again to my creative expression. I was unprepared for the beautiful gift of awakening that resulted from this simple intention and how this session would contribute toward continued clarity related to my Divine purpose.

After the shoot, I watched the pictures appear one by one on the computer screen. I felt my inner judge/critic poised for action, so I took a deep breath and relaxed into my intention to simply be present and let the images unfold. As I maintained a gentle attentiveness, I watched as different aspects of myself emerged on the screen. I paid attention to the feelings and desires that were awakening within me as I gazed at the multitude of images. As I watched, I saw parts of myself appear and generate strong feelings related to my innermost desires. I began to get in touch with the archetypes, the templates that served as mythical glue connecting it all: feelings, desires and images. With each click of the mouse a new energy greeted me. I watched in wonder as parts of me that had been dormant for years shone forth, sharing important realizations. In wonderment I experienced pieces of my life love story emerging to re-awaken inner previously forgotten intentions.

From one image, the Eternal Child appeared. I saw her innocence and joy shining from the picture. She was silently inviting me to play, modeling an eternal connection to youthfulness in mind, body and spirit. As I attended to her presence, I was aware of my shadow side of the struggling to accept the aging process. This archetype cringed at the recognition of new wrinkles apparent in the photos. I also saw her recent triumph from dependency on others for survival needs and well-being to independence and began celebrating her development. And, finally, I realized that her gentle image was a reminder to embrace the playful side of life, remembering that all my needs are always met. Another picture brought forth the Artist. I felt a deep urge to express my art, an animation with wanting to share and give birth to continuous creative flow. The Artist invited me to express, express, express, freely and openly without fear or judgment.

The Magical/Innocent Child jumped from behind another photo. I immediately recalled the "once upon a time" stories from my childhood and wondered how I had possibly forgotten some of my vivid dreams over the years. She smiled and asked me to remember, to embrace the dreams now, allowing my personal love story with life to simply unfold with ease and grace. Flow and possibility are always present, she reminded me. Allow yourself to embrace the endless power of your imagination.

A certain expression, an intense look in a photo activated within me the Warrior, the huntress Artemis, who was challenging me to point my arrows of creative energy and direct their mark. She reminded me of the importance of moving forward with direction, suggesting that I mobilize my forces of focus, intention and follow-through.

Finally, as the three hundred odd photos were nearing the end of their parade across the screen, I caught a glimpse of the Nurturing Mother, her gaze filled with unconditional love and acceptance. Her love poured forth, showing an immense acceptance and surrender for "what is" and trust that all is complete, whole and cared for in Spirit. She was showing me the vast capacity for love that exists in me, in everyone and how, when directed at every aspect of my life, it brings ultimate peace in every moment.

This experience brought me a deeper sense of my Divine purpose and renewed dedication to It. All these messages were next steps linked to the development and realization of my intention. I learned that a simple glimpse and willingness to embrace all parts of oneself through activation of the witness further opened me to a greater sense of well-being and clarity. My intention, while initially simple and seemingly small, carried with it the depth of message and love for the unfolding of the next chapter of my life.

These pictures keep on giving, changing and emerging, showing me different aspects of myself as I am open to them. As I periodically re-visit the images and stay open to my feelings, allowing the innermost desires to pour forth, I am awakened to the archetypical messages contained within them. What a gift to be awakened to guidance that encourages the further acceptance of your own mythical love story. What a gift to experience the surrendering that allows the expansive living of it.

creating a new life story

What old story are you holding onto about yourself that removes you from embracing and expressing the magnificent, whole and powerful person that you are? What set of beliefs are you feeding that give away your power? It's imperative, on a daily basis, that we build enough strength to overcome the old stories that keep us small, thus making safe choices that don't come close to expressing our God-given potential.

In my late twenties I began experiencing various degrees of pain in my lower back. I have no doubt that part of the reason for this physical pain was due to the deep emotional pain I was experiencing at that time in my life. My mother was dying of cancer and my wife had just left our marriage. I felt deeply deserted and riddled with self-judgment. I felt weak at my core and my back literally did not feel as if it could support me.

As I gradually healed from that experience, the back pain lessened. Over the years, the degree of pain has fluctuated depending upon my level of exercise, stress and the lifting of heavy objects. A few years ago I began to experience deeper consistent pain than in the past, perhaps due to the body's aging. It wasn't going away, to the degree of becoming a bit debilitating, making it difficult to bend over and do basic daily functions.

I've always prided myself in being flexible, associating flexibility with being vital, expressive, alive and adventurous. This degree of stiffness simply did not fit my picture of who Carl is, so I gradually became more willing to commit to a weekly regimen of stretching. I began to recognize that it was necessary to devote a couple days a week to stretching and strengthening the muscles in my back.

As I devoted myself to this new practice, my back began to feel stronger and the pain decreased. My back was teaching me that a new and deeper listening to my body's needs was now required. I began to learn that as my body continues to age, I couldn't expect it to hold its strength without continuing to build its muscle growth.

In time, the need for two days of stretching became three, then every other day, and currently I stretch daily. I honestly cannot boast that I embrace this daily ritual with bold enthusiasm, but I recognize that if I don't make it a daily practice, my body becomes stiffer with pain.

Recently, I was in the middle of a deep backstretch and my emotions wanted to have the best of me. They were screaming out, "This is just too hard, too painful! You don't deserve to be in this much pain! You're just not strong enough to handle this discomfort. Stop now and save yourself from any further pain and struggle. You're just too weak to handle this!"

Does any of this limiting self-talk sound familiar? While in the midst of this inner dialogue of doom, I caught myself and pieced together that if I listened to and acted on this persuasive train of thought, I would experience greater pain and debilitation in the long run. I became so clear that even though the stretching can feel painful, in reality it's building strength throughout my body. The real question became, what story am I entertaining and how am I interpreting this sensation while stretching? It's truly my choice as to how I experience what I'm calling pain while in this daily practice. I have the ability to just as easily associate this sensation that I've labeled "painful" as a positive, burning pulsation that is building strength, vitality and aliveness throughout my entire body.

In order to effectively do this, I must be willing to let go of any vestiges of victimhood, any old associations with the false belief that anything or anyone has power over me. I must be willing in that moment of limiting self-talk to challenge it and say, "No, these thoughts and feelings are simply not true! They may be very familiar, but they are not true. What's true is that I am strong, healthy and vital, and these exercises are really good for me. They are making me even stronger as my muscles are being honored through the burning sensation that's taking place."

This ability to catch and challenge old beliefs *(along with the feelings that surface as a result of these beliefs)* is imperative if we wish to claim power over our lives. Rev. Dr. Michael Bernard Beckwith, author of *Spiritual Liberation*, coined a phrase that I've held most useful over the years. He says, "The pain pushes until the vision pulls." In my case, the pain that was pushing was located in my back and the vision that was being asked to step forward was a deeper conviction in knowing that every part of me is strong, vital and healthy.

My body fully supports me as I fully honor and support my body. And perhaps the pain that was pushing was not just the back pain. Perhaps it was also the pain of holding onto old beliefs that reinforced feeling small and fragile, feeling scared to play full out for fear of being ridiculed or judged.

What areas of your life are causing pain and what vision wishes to be cultivated and expressed? Where are you holding onto fear-based beliefs that are holding you back? Take a moment right now, close your eyes and ask yourself:

- What pain is pushing me right now?

- What vision desires to birth and express through me at this time?

Whatever clarity comes forward must be honored through your day-to-day willingness to move through the pain by challenging it and making choices that support your growth, your expansion and your building of strength at your inner core. The answer is NEVER "out there somewhere." It's not, as I mentioned before, found in the right job, the perfect mate, looking like a supermodel, being successful through others' standards, driving the right car, having a higher education, or in any way of being that's not guided by your inner compass.

Each time that your picture is being taken, you can ask yourself, "Am I resting comfortably in my unique, radiant essence or am I looking outside myself at a false image of who I think I should be?"

If the answer is the latter, take a moment to close your eyes and feel the presence that emanates from your center.

Allow that energy of expression that is like no other to fully bubble up to the surface and greet the camera with great honor and light, as if you're greeting your dearest friend.

Right now is that essential moment. Every "still frame" of your life is beckoning you forward to play full out, to let your brilliant light shine like no other. Your rich contributions are so deeply needed and valued in our world. The more fully that you embrace each moment's click of your life, the more that you will continue to explode into fuller hues of color reflecting the rich expression of your radiance. Like the majestic eagle, you will find yourself soaring gracefully above life's circumstances with crystal-clear vision, steering your direction wisely while embodying the wisdom that serves your grandest of purpose and the fullest of expression in your truest of service to the world.

Snapshot Memories

By Donna DeNomme

Suck in your gut, my father would say when taking my picture. Being a smaller-framed child, my belly was way out of proportion for my size. As one naturally gifted with a good eye for a likeable picture, he was just trying to help…yet, with an already shaky sense of self, I grew to be someone who never felt good enough whenever I was being photographed. Maybe if I just hold my breath and smile, it will come out all right. Well, usually it didn't. I had stacks and stacks of photo albums, and it was rare to find a photo of me that I saw in a positive light; others remarked about it too. I just did not photograph well.

So it was with reservation that I arrived for my brief photo shoot. We had only a small window, as I was one of many during this special day of professional photos for my organization. We began quickly. ICK, that all-familiar feeling was very present—can I hope to get maybe just one that will be decent? It wasn't the photographer's ability that I doubted; it was mine. After a few quick *shots*—aptly named as each one penetrated my heart, deep to the core, where wounds live—Carl suggested how I should sit: lean forward, turn your head, chin up (*yuck, this always intensifies the terror*). Piercing my negative mind chatter infiltrated one potent word, "Beautiful." I looked up to see this sweet face beaming at me with acceptance, "Yes, this is going to work." He seemed to believe what he was saying. Click. Click. I stopped sweating. Click. Click. Click. "Come on, Donna, show me what you've got. Shine!" Click. "Say, yes!" Click. Click. Click. "That's right, let your light shine. Yes!" Click. Click. Click. Click. Click. Moments blended together until he said, "Great. We've got it." That's it, I thought, we're done? Oh, my, not only was that not so painful, but dare I say, I may have enjoyed it? Out of an entire roll of thirty-six, there were only two shots that were passable (*my previous criteria for acceptance*) and thirty-four were fabulous! Who'd have believed it?

Since I can remember, I have always been fascinated with the way that people understand themselves and the world around them. My capacity for self-reflection is fairly evolved; yet, surprisingly, a photographer with his well-developed eye was able to place a light in a particular place with a particular angle, which illumined a shadow before hidden and unaddressed. "Not good enough" was enlivened by "show me you" and "let your light shine." In that one photo shoot, a strong lifelong belief that my truest essence could not be captured, that I could not be positively seen, was changed forever. I opened my eyes to the beauty that had beforehand been captive in that dark, unknown space. It is this authentic beauty that I tap into now when I am being photographed. Instead of trying to look or be a certain way, I am very simply shining the light of my own authentic being. "You are so photogenic," I often hear now. Perhaps, and, at our essence level, aren't we all?

As an author and speaker, I necessarily update my promotional photos from time to time, but gone are the days of countless photo albums. I find it ironic that I no longer feel a need to collect them. Now that I am more comfortable with authentically expressing what is inside of me and bringing it fully present to the outer world, I do not need a camera lens to document that for me. "Oh, tonight I have the perfect outfit on—let's get a picture!" has evolved to "I feel glorious tonight!" I savor life as it is happening. I am able to call forth, in my mind's eye as inner snapshots; no longer dependent on an outer physical thing for validation, these moments of completion live inside of me. Photos have value, certainly, yet the understanding of a precious moment in time goes far beyond a glossy 8 x 10.

Life is paradoxical. Surely we travel a solo journey and we still need each other as catalysts for our deepening. Understanding isn't measured by education, or life experience...in an instant someone can say or do something that can literally change our destiny. In a moment of pure acceptance and vivid reflection, click, my inner beauty was set free. She is now often seen dancing with childlike abandon...and loving life!

the outer reflecting the inner

Looking to outer circumstances to determine how we're doing in our lives, or how we're feeling in the moment, is an epidemic in our culture. I have to constantly catch myself when I begin to travel down this conditioned path that can only lead to comparison, self-judgment and an overall sense of misery and depression. It seems that most of us, to one degree or another, have been deeply influenced by this belief *(unless of course you grew up in a cave or an ashram or had enlightened parents that home-schooled you and kept you from the outside world's influence).*

When you stop and think about it, it's pretty amazing that we can function as a culture with any semblance of harmony living with this misnomer. It's no wonder that so many of us feel depressed, lost and without a strong sense of purpose. From studying a wide spectrum of teachings from throughout the ages and through my own great trial and error, I've learned that our inner experience always shapes our outer circumstances! If my thoughts and beliefs are deeply anchored in knowing that this is a safe and abundant Universe, overflowing with riches and resources that support me, my physical world cannot help but reflect this flow of prosperity. The perfect people and opportunities that support my greatest of expression will continue to show up in my life because I'm certain that this is how the Universe operates.

In my late twenties, I had the opportunity to spend a day with noted futurist and inventor Buckminster Fuller at an event entitled "Integrity Day." Bucky was a mathematical genius. He knew how the laws of physics apply to the structural laws of the Universe, and how this structural integrity applies to our everyday lives. He spoke with passion and certainty about these principles. Even though I didn't rationally understand a large percentage of what he was saying, there was something within me that truly gained a greater insight into the interconnectedness of all things and the integral wisdom that lies at the center of all consciousness, from the smallest sub-particle to the vastness of the infinite galaxies.

Bucky shared a personal story that continues to influence my life to this day. He spoke about his need to follow his inner directive, his inner calling. As a young adult, he stayed true to listening within and being guided. Inspiration abounded and many powerful insights and inventions were birthed during this period. As his family grew, there came a point when friends convinced him that he needed to get a "real job" that would provide a stable income for his wife and children. He caved in to the influence around him and temporarily got a steady job, thinking that this would be a more responsible choice for all concerned.

During this period, he battled severe depression and thoughts of suicide. He described it as the darkest time of his life. Once he let go of the job and went back to his life's work, he felt re-inspired and on purpose. Ideas, inventions and passionate purpose began to flourish and he was back in sync with the larger purpose for his life. He pointed out that for most of his life he was often living on the financial edge, not knowing when the next payment would come in to handle needed expenses. Yet the Universe always ended up providing all needs for him and his family.

At eighty-two years of age, looking back on his vast career and his most enriching life, Buckminster Fuller assured me *(along with all others in the room)* that it's not only okay but encouraged to follow my unique path and to trust that it will always support and uplift me. Here was a wise and respected elder who I've held as a profound role model throughout my career that has always mirrored back the need to be true to my highest purpose, especially in times of doubt and fear.

Whenever we're feeling confused, frustrated or unhappy with life's circumstances, it's imperative that we stop and examine what core beliefs are running their endless loop in our daily thought patterns. Some of these might sound like, "I never seem to get ahead as there's only enough money to take care of bare essentials," or "I never seem to attract a relationship that supports and honors me," or "My body is never fully healthy because I'm too susceptible to getting other people's germs."

Can you see how your outer world would naturally say, "Yes, you're right!" if you are constantly reinforcing these directives? The trick is learning how to catch these irrational patterns as they arise and then challenge them to a duel! But your blade must be quite sharp and your maneuvering skill and dexterity must be quick and decisive. Otherwise, the old, conditioned belief will be stronger because it's had many years to gain weight and familiarity with your day-to-day way of operating. It has become quite fit, cunning and muscular and it will convince you that it's right unless you learn how to take the upper hand.

You must become so engaged in fine-tuning your reception to the degree that you're able to consciously hear the "broadcast of lies" each time that they come across the airwaves of your mind. You then get to switch stations to "The Enlightened Channel," it's K N O W on the dial! On this station, all transmissions remind you of your true gifts and the perfection of the Universe operating through you in every moment.

In recent years, I've witnessed more and more experiences that validate the theory that our inner visions create our outer reality. During my morning meditations when my mind is still, I'll occasionally be given a vivid image for a portrait. I've learned that when I don't resist thoughts floating through my awareness while meditating, there can often be wonderful gems that are offered.

One morning while in meditation, I saw *(and felt)* a vivid image of Deepak Chopra. When I say that I saw and felt the image, that's exactly what took place. It's as if the feeling created the visual internal image. The feeling was one of sacred presence being illuminated. The image that burst forth in my mind immediately following the feeling depicts Deepak emerging out of the darkness and illuminating his surroundings with a glowing candle in his hands.

Once my mind became conscious of this image, I smiled and felt deep gratitude for being given this visual gift. When I completed my meditation, I wrote about the experience. It made complete sense to my rational mind because I see Deepak as a messenger of light through his most illuminating life's work. He truly brings the light of consciousness to the world and his teachings have sparked significant insights throughout my life.

Imagine the rich storehouse of information awaiting you as you simply still the mind and listen. When you're not invested in trying to figure things out or make something happen, your inner directive takes over and always guides you onto your perfect path. However, it can appear to be paradoxical, for if you're purposely meditating in order to reach a certain result, the mind is not truly being still. You must let go of all investments and sincerely rest in the stillness without any agenda, simply honoring the wisdom that prevails beyond your human mind. You are being called to trust that there is a higher intelligence always directing your choices as you let go and listen.

If you're not happy with any of your outer circumstances, perhaps it's time to give any remnants of fear, doubt, control and judgment over to the grand depository of the Divine! As you're willing to let go of these old habitual patterns, you begin to surrender into the "peace that passes all human understanding" and gradually it feels more comfortable to rest in the stillness. When the stillness becomes more comfortable than the outer chatter, you'll know that you're on the path that will only bring you clarity, inspired vision and deep fulfillment.

Guiding Light

By Sharon Hampton

On a beautiful Colorado morning blanketed in snow, clear blue sky, bright sun, tree limbs encased in ice, I took a walk alone with my camera in Chatfield State Park to find what I could see. My digital SLR has served our family well in illustrating new life, sacred celebrations and daily adventures. However, during one of the quietest mornings I have ever heard, I discovered that the images taken were not doing justice to the beauty of the given moment. I felt it was time to switch from auto mode to manual mode and to learn how to best utilize the options my camera has to offer. Since that day, I have learned that, to fully understand how a camera operates, one must understand the concepts of aperture and shutter speed involving focus, light and time.

Aperture affects a picture in two ways and is referenced as F stop on the camera. The first way aperture plays a role is that it changes the depth of field of a picture. Depth of field deals with how much of an image is in focus. The larger the F stop the greater the depth of field, while a smaller F stop produces a smaller depth of field. Both offer their benefits, sometimes depicting the big picture, other times focusing in on a very specific image. The second function of aperture is to control the amount of light that can enter the camera through the shutter opening.

As with aperture, shutter speed affects the amount of light that enters the camera by controlling the duration of time that the sensor is exposed to light. A fast shutter speed is great for an action shot because it allows light in for a short amount of time. A slow shutter speed will allow light in for a longer period of time, adding clarity to a picture. In other words, slowing down and allowing light in can make for a clearer, more vivid image.

The more I gave thought to these terms and concepts, the more they resonated with me, likened to my current spiritual experience. Aperture left me considering my focus in life, at this time of my life, in light of all I can see. Focusing in on the bigger picture has allowed me to see the endless possibilities to this life journey with greater clarity. Shutter speed brought to mind how much light, being God or Spirit, I would allow into my individual image. The more I have opened up my mind and heart, the greater my exposure to new thought; the more time devoted to practice, the greater my resolution. Just as a photographer can shift from auto mode to manual and influence the process of co-creating an image with a camera, so can we co-create with Spirit. It is within the time of quiet stillness that we are able to realign with Spirit, release aspects of the human ego and find true peace that lies only within the soul. It is here that we also find grace. To know grace is to know God. In looking through the lens, by determining our focus through our thoughts, spiritual beliefs and practices while allowing the guiding light of Spirit into our open hearts, we can develop a clearer image of an authentic life.

you are the light

In the Bible it is written, "You are the light." Throughout history, there have been countless interpretations of this passage. Perhaps it's intended to be broad and ambiguous in its meaning. I choose to see humankind as vessels or containers of light and quantum physics is now recognizing that light is actually a form of consciousness.

The metaphors are endless. "I was blind, but now I see." It is in the light that we literally see and metaphorically where we gain insight. One might say, "In the light of clarity, I now know which direction to take in my life." We generally sleep in darkness, allowing our body and mind to rest and replenish, and in the light of day we awaken and give of our gifts that are fueled by the light.

The word inspiration is derived from the Greek word, *inspirit*, which literally translates as being one with Spirit, or being infused with the light of the Divine. When we're inspired, we feel deeply alive, enthusiastic and fueled by a strong sense of purpose. On the opposite end of the spectrum, we generally feel depressed when our choices appear limited and when we're not tapped into a deep sense of purpose or connection to what truly fuels our soul.

One of the most basic formulas or road maps for being successful and feeling fulfilled in life lies in our moment-to-moment choice to fully let in the light, allowing it to guide, sustain and spark every thought, word, feeling and activity. This simple measure lies at the heart of deepening our faith.

I know that my faith continues to broaden as I more fully recognize and embrace the power of the light—in, throughout and as my very life. It is when I'm completely receptive to this radiance that I feel I can move mountains. This is when I'm the most alive and directed to unconditionally offer my gifts and talents with great joy and gusto. When inspired vision is flowing, there's a sense of grand adventure that's being navigated by a pureness of heart.

Below is an affirmative statement that I encourage you to read daily with deep conviction and feeling:

As the light guides every thought, feeling and choice in my life, all effort and struggle is released. I am living in the radiant flow of the pure creative spark that birthed me to be...like no one else. I am fully ignited and guided in every moment and my most valued gifts are being brilliantly refined and shared with the world. Truly, every click of my life is that essential moment of letting go into the Yes, into the Tao. This very moment is my life-governing choice point and I choose to live with a pureness of heart while embracing every single frame of my most treasured and gifted life.

We are all inherently drawn to the light, for that is what we are, the very stuff that we are made of. As an example, I arrived home one evening to find hundreds of tiny gnats circling a kitchen light. My first response was one of disgust, feeling like our kitchen had been invaded by a platoon of microscopic soldiers.

I assessed the surroundings and concluded that they clearly were small enough to fit through the screen of our opened kitchen window. For a few moments, I felt helpless, not knowing an ecologically sound way to get rid of these minute pests *(I don't believe I've owned a can of bug spray in my entire adult life, as my preference is to find a healthier and natural solution).*

It then dawned on me that if in fact they infested our kitchen because they were drawn to the light, I could simple light a new path for them and eventually direct them out of the house. What a simple remedy! In that moment, my inner light bulb of ingenuity switched on and I created a light trail for them straight out the backdoor!

Mind you, it took a bit of time as I needed to turn off all other lights in the house and selectively turn one on at a time, finally leading to the backyard light, leaving the door open so they could *(similar to how they arrived)* travel through the screen and thus swarm around the outdoor bulb until daybreak. My wife arrived home while in the midst of carrying out this light-orchestrated exodus and fortunately put up with limited light in the house for the remainder of the evening. She endearingly referred to me as the Pied Piper!

How about being a Pied Piper of light in your world! What is it in your life that illumines you and fills you with inspired vision? As you more fully open to your inner-light, you will become and serve as a beacon of inspiration in your daily affairs and dealings.

Imagine standing in front of a camera and simply beaming the light right into the core of the camera's aperture! What tangible presence would be shining through with each picture taken? Everyone *(including yourself)* viewing those pictures would be ignited with the radiance. Your face would glow with the light of consciousness and your image would truly serve as a reminder, as a spark of inspired vision. You would be a reflection of light, a unique and radiant expression of both individualized and collective consciousness. Like a perfectly cut diamond that reflects back multidimensional facets of light, this is the genuine truth of your nature.

You are the light… **CLICK**…

Let it shine… **CLICK**…

Right now… **CLICK**…

You are perfect… **CLICK**….

Contributors

Kenny Loggins: Kenny Loggins is a two-time Grammy award winning singer-songwriter whose superstar career has traversed diverse styles on record and in film music. Loggins' creative journey has encompassed over three decades of hit singles and more than twelve albums exceeding platinum status. Throughout his career, Kenny has demonstrated a consistent, strong and powerful commitment to the environment. From Earth Day to green energy, to global warming, to children's health, Loggins has been at the forefront of sustainability and over the decades has become a respected thought leader on environmental change.

Carol Ratcliffe Alm: A coveted strengths-based executive and personal coach, successful business strategist and acclaimed presenter, Carol Ratcliffe Alm is highly regarded for her coaching outcomes, strategy results and powerful presentations. With more than thirty years in corporate leadership and her consulting practice, she optimizes the talent of individuals and organizations through her presence, skill and the insight of her experience. She has served as Senior Vice President of the Gallup Organization and Associate Dean of the Daniels College of Business at University of Denver. She may be reached at carol@carolalm.com.

Kathleen McGowan: Kathleen McGowan is the *New York Times* Best-selling Author of *The Magdalene Line* series and *The Source of Miracles*. Her books have sold over a million copies and are published in almost forty languages while appearing in over seventy countries. Kathleen McGowan hosts *The Spirit Revolution* on BBS Radio with her partner, author Philip Coppens. www.KathleenMcGowan.com.

Cynthia James: Cynthia James is a transformational specialist guiding thousands of people to make changes at a spiritual level for lasting healing in their lives. She is the award-winning author of *What Will Set You Free*, and sought-after lecturer, teacher and internationally renowned performing artist. Cynthia is a featured guide in the movie *Leap!*, the personal growth guide for the GaiamLife Community and featured on numerous radio programs. She's facilitated hundreds of workshops and seminars, co-hosted a talk show in Los Angeles and has been a featured speaker in business and spiritual forums.

Ram Dass: Ram Dass is a spiritual teacher and social activist committed to serving humanity. He has a PhD in Psychology from Stanford and taught at Harvard, U.C. Berkeley and Stanford from 1958 to 1963. He was one of the forerunners of psychedelic research from 1961 until 1967. Then he met his spiritual teacher, Neem Karoli Baba, who was adept at yoga and spiritual philosophy. Since 1967, Ram Dass has been involved in a range of service projects and has authored and coauthored fourteen books.

Leilani Raashida Henry: Leilani Henry is a demonstrated leader in the fields of workplace culture, creativity and wellness. She is the founder of Being & Living Enterprises, and creator of Brain Jewels®, a multi-sensory transformation process. Her fellowship from Regis University's Institute on the Common Good recognizes and honors her work in mind-body connection and dialogue for organizational change. She is cited in national publications and organizations such as *Corporate Meetings & Incentives*, *Fast Company*, *Fetzer Institute* and *New Visions in Business*. Find out more at www.beingandliving.com. Follow Leilani on Twitter@beandlive.

Karen Drucker: Karen Drucker has recorded thirteen CDs of her original positive-message music and has also written an inspirational book, *Let Go of the Shore: Stories and Songs That Set the Spirit Free*. She sings, speaks and leads workshops at women's retreats, conferences, and various churches around the country. Karen is also known as a "music weaver" at spiritual conferences alongside authors such as Alan Cohen, Joan Borysenko, Debbie Ford and many others. Karen has been called "a master of communicating presence and spirituality through music." She loves making music, making a difference and touching hearts.

Dr. Joe Dispenza: Neuroscientist, lecturer and author Joe Dispenza, D.C., is an expert on the brain, mind and human potential. He has taught thousands of people around the world how they can re-program their thinking and eliminate self-destructive habits so they can reach their goals and visions. He draws on both scientific and universal principles to deliver practical tools and techniques that empower people to truly change from the inside. Dr. Joe is the author of the bestselling book *Evolve Your Brain: The Science of Changing Your Mind* and was also featured in the movie, *What the BLEEP Do We Know!?*

Dan Kessler: Dan Kessler produced and edited *The Stars of David Jewish Science Fiction Volume One* in 1996. He moved from Los Angeles in 2003 to the gorgeous wine country north of San Francisco. Dan is developing a new Internet series, *The StarsofDavidGalaxy12*, and writing a novel titled *Lembert Dome*, his West Los Angeles autobiography fantasy. He owns a financial services company, practices Bikram Yoga, enjoys Landmark Education classes, live music, picnics, hiking, exploring country roads, and is passionate about inspiring others to become their most empowered self.

Raymond Aaron: Raymond Aaron, *New York Times* Best-selling Author, teaches you how to double your income doing what you love. To attend a workshop, please register at www.aaron.com.

Tom Robbins: Tom Robbins is the author of nine off-beat but popular novels, a best-selling story collection and numerous articles and essays. His work is published in twenty-two languages.

Marian Head: Marian is the award-winning author of *Revolutionary Agreements: Twelve Ways to Transform Stress of Struggle into Freedom and Joy* (www.RevolutionaryAgreements.com). She and her husband Glenn are entrepreneurs who engage people in making a living by making a difference.

Zemirah Jazwierska: Zemirah Jazwierska awakened to a new life perspective when she encountered The Science of Mind at Mile Hi Church in Lakewood, Colorado, and began to practice the spiritual principles. She currently is expanding her creative expression to inspire children, families and educators with joyful relaxation techniques and mindfulness practice. Her work can be found at www.kidsrelaxation.com.

Donna DeNomme: Donna DeNomme is a role model for using life challenges as opportunities to propel oneself into an extraordinary life. Coming from a background of brutal sexual abuse, which led to rebellious adolescent gang affiliation, single motherhood and state welfare, she knew first-hand how self-defeating life can be… Donna shares comfort, encouragement, and inspirational strategies for empowered, conscious living. She is the award-winning, internationally published author of *Turtle Wisdom: Coming Home to Yourself* and *Ophelia's Oracle: Discovering the Healthy, Happy, Self-Aware, and Confident Girl in the Mirror.* www.inlightenedsource.com and www.opheliasoracle.com

Sharon Hampton: Sharon D. Hampton lives in Littleton, Colorado, with her husband and family.

Endorsement Contributors

Joan Borysenko, PhD, is one of the leading experts on stress, spirituality and the mind/body connection. She has a doctorate in medical sciences from Harvard Medical School, and is a licensed clinical psychologist. A *New York Times* bestselling author and blogger for *The Huffington Post*, her work has appeared in newspapers ranging from *The Washington Post* to *The Wall Street Journal*. A warm and engaging teacher who speaks worldwide, she blends cutting-edge science and psychology with a profound and palpable sense of the sacred (and a world-class sense of humor). Joan lives in the mountains of Colorado with her husband, Gordon Dveirin. You can find out more about her work, watch videos and read articles at www.joanborysenko.com.

For the past four decades, **John Bradshaw** has combined his exceptional skills in the role of counselor, author, management consultant, theologian, philosopher and public speaker, becoming one of the leading figures in the fields of addiction/recovery, family systems, relationships, spiritual and emotional growth and management training. His dynamic training and therapies are practiced all over the world. He is the author of such major bestsellers as *Family Secrets, Healing the Shame That Binds You, Homecoming, and Creating Love*. He lives in Houston, Texas, and gives lectures and workshops nationwide. Learn more about John at www.johnbradshaw.com.

Jack Canfield is the co-author of the #1 *New York Times* best-selling *Chicken Soup for the Soul* series, which has sold more than 500 million copies in 47 languages. He is a featured teacher in the movies *The Secret* and *Tapping the Source*; and has appeared on more than 1000 radio and television programs. Jack is also the CEO of the Canfield Training Group and the founder of the Transformational Leadership Council. He lives with his wife, Inga, in Santa Barbara, California. Website: www.JackCanfield.com.

Katherine Woodward Thomas is the national bestselling author of *Calling in "The One"*; a transformative educator; licensed psychotherapist; and the co-creator and co-leader, along with teaching partner Claire Zammit, of the Feminine Power transformative courses and the Feminine Power Global Community, a thriving learning community serving women worldwide. Katherine is a creative and inspired transformative educator with nearly 20 years of experience designing and facilitating seminars and programs that support the emergence of life-altering shifts in consciousness, both individually and collectively. Website: www.CallingInTheOne.net.

Lynne Twist is a global activist, fundraiser, speaker, consultant and author. Lynne has dedicated her life to global initiatives that serve the best instincts in all of us. She has raised hundreds of millions of dollars and trained thousands of fundraisers to be more effective in their work. Lynne has spent more than three decades working in positions of leadership with many global initiatives including: ending world hunger; protecting the world's rainforests; empowering indigenous peoples; improving health, economic, and political conditions for women and children; advancing the scientific understanding of human consciousness and creating a sustainable future for all life. Visit: www.SoulofMoney.org.

About the Author

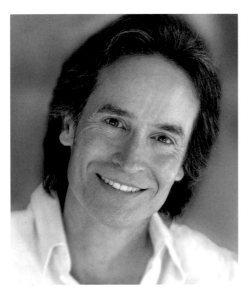

Born and raised in Los Angeles, Carl Studna is a multifaceted photographer/videographer, lecturer, author, spiritual counselor and transformational leader. Carl's three decades of intimate portraits of influential people ranging from the Dalai Lama to Paul McCartney are known worldwide and have graced publications ranging from *Time* magazine to *Rolling Stone*.

Carl's mission is to inspire, educate and strengthen self-esteem in others through cultivating a safe and loving environment that fosters a genuine experience of perfection and grace residing at the core of our being, thus allowing true essence to shine.

The primary theme that weaves its way through Carl's lectures, interviews and published works is that life is a sacred journey to be cherished and embraced, awakening to the splendor that lies in life's seemingly ordinary moments. Through Carl's photographs, these moments are witnessed in the vulnerable presence between soul mates, in the warm glow of the setting sun as it backlights a golden aspen leaf whose edges glisten from its snow-laced frosting, from the pure wonder, grace and intelligence of a newborn baby's eyes, and in the simple "let go" of a face that's allowing its true self to simply be seen in the purity of its essential beauty and perfection.

Carl holds a Master's degree in Spiritual Psychology, and is a licensed "Science of Mind" Practitioner and a member of the Transformational Leadership Council. Currently residing in the pristine mountains of Colorado with his wife Cynthia and their two dogs, Carl views the world as his home and considers it an honor to travel the globe in offering his talent and his gifts.